Mapping
St. Louis History:

An Exhibition of Historic Maps, Rare Books and Images
Commemorating the 250th Anniversary of the Founding of St. Louis

Mapping St. Louis

An Exhibition of Historic Maps,

History:

Rare Books and Images Commemorating the 250th Anniversary of the Founding of St. Louis

by John Neal Hoover

with an Introduction by Peter J. Kastor

St. Louis Mercantile Library at
the University of Missouri–St. Louis

2014

The Mercantile Library is grateful for the generous support of Michael Buehler, Boston Rare Maps; Blackford F. Brauer, Hunter Engineering; Don Cresswell, Philadelphia Print Shop; Paul and Judith Haudrich; Murray Hudson; Bruce McKittrick Rare Books; Harry Newman, the Old Print Shop, and to an anonymous donor in making this publication possible.

Published in the United States of America
by the
St. Louis Mercantile Library
University of Missouri–St. Louis
1 University Boulevard
St. Louis, Missouri 63121
©2014 by the Curators of the University of Missouri

Hoover, John Neal
Mapping St. Louis history : an exhibition of historic maps, rare books and images
commemorating the 250th anniversary of the founding of St. Louis / by John N. Hoover ;
introduction by Peter Kastor. – St. Louis, Mo. : St. Louis Mercantile Library, University
of Missouri–St. Louis, 2014.
p.: col. ill., maps ; cm.
Includes bibliographical references and index.
1. Saint Louis (Mo.) – History
2. Saint Louis (Mo.) – Maps
3. Chouteau, Auguste, 1750-1829
4. Laclède–Liguest, Pierre de, 1724-1778
I. Kastor, Peter J.
F474.S2H77 2014
ISBN 978-0-9802002-6-3

Design and Typesetting: Patricia Archer
Photography: August Jennewein
Printer: World Press, Inc.
Printed and bound in the United States of America
Typeface: Liberty, Cambria

Mapping
St. Louis History

Dedicated to the past, present, and future staff of the Mercantile Library
who have been, are, or I am sure will be, map lovers all.

Foreword

St. Louis in Maps and Mapping St. Louis

Early French, Spanish and English explorers and travelers referred to the St. Louis region as the finest confluence of natural waterways in the world. Traders and settlers of the first town on the site of modern day St. Louis considered the area a perfect harbor, the best along the river for thousands of miles. Modern airline pilots can't seem to resist, if authorized to do so by the traffic control tower, showing their passengers an eastern approach of the Mississippi and the great city which looms ahead in such surprising majesty, never do they tire of this scene. What we see today on maps of the big bend in the Mississippi, people for centuries have seen—endless possibilities in business, trade, wealth, growth, in working and living.

The St. Louis Mercantile Library possesses an extraordinary collection of maps, charts, plats and plans, atlases and loose folded sheets spanning the world, some centuries old, and some very recently printed and acquired. The early merchants who founded the Mercantile Library in young St. Louis were great map collectors, especially of the region, the newly opening American West, and the trade ways to Asia. James Yeatman, for example, the founder of the Mercantile, was a merchant and investor in many civic trading projects related to bringing the goods of the world to the city's doorstep, and among the great folios he donated were large atlases of hard to obtain charts and plans spanning the globe.

That early collection became the springboard in later times for the Library to become a research storehouse for maps and plans from across the nation, and particularly the area. When a new city map was published, it came to the old reference room; when a plan for the streets or a subdivision was newly laid out, those charts were often donated to the Mercantile by city and county officials of the day.

Years ago I set about working with the maps here when time allowed. I wanted to collect one map of both Missouri and of St. Louis for every year of their existence, if possible. A lot has been done with that collection and we have stuck tenaciously to our quixotic goal, when given the mystery and scarcity of eighteenth century St. Louis maps actually having survived, and the current trend to do away with paper, in deference to rapidly changing, immediately revisable digital copies. Today the collection comprises many thousands of maps for the use of researchers worldwide, not just about St. Louis, but for the history of the broader world the Mercantile has always been known to collect. Locally, we have added hundreds of maps and identified and re-catalogued many others into a special collection which can now help lead in future years, hopefully, a community effort to create a thorough digital library of our region's maps and a fuller list of all known holdings of the vast heritage in maps which are preserved in archives and libraries across St. Louis, not just at the Mercantile.

Traditionally it is daunting to deal with maps in libraries. They have special storage concerns and unusual rules for cataloguing. To exhibit them takes a great amount of space and time for special handling; however, the 250th Anniversary of the founding of St. Louis seemed a very appropriate time for the Mercantile to prepare this catalogue and the accompanying exhibition in marking the heritage and influence of the mapped environment of St. Louis through the ages. The goal of this exhibition is to show the range of maps for our region, from the earliest explorers' maps present here—indeed long before St. Louis was founded by Laclède and the Chouteaus—through territorial maps of Missouri, to the relentless march of St. Louis city history as seen on one map of the town after another, through the generations.

This catalogue is thus a guide for future researchers and our staff as we build digital resources for the Library's map collection. The major known St. Louis maps have been digitally scanned and preserved, inventoried, framed, matted, foldered and flattened —rediscovered— as a byproduct of an exhibition which will allow the viewer to become more familiar with the vast range of attention mapmakers, planning officials and surveyors have always given the St. Louis area. The city was an early model for the growth of the urban environment out of the frontier forest, and maps help to tell that story in ways few other historical resources can.

Maps have a way of reporting accurately a landscape, a town, a city. They are used of course, for the traveler to find one's way around, physically. But even the most detailed, matter-of-fact reference maps, depending on the time they were published or for the place or purpose they described, can have another purpose—to excite the imagination, to influence the world they describe. Maps document, as well as cause and create change. St. Louis' maps were and are no exception to this circumstance, and they help to show where the city has been and where it will be going in the next 250 years. They possess a power transcendent to the paper and ink that they come from, and the St. Louis Mercantile Library is proud to offer the story of its region and city through these special treasures. The city's heritage moves and breathes through them, from the early French empire of Louisiana and the awareness in early times of a great North American river confluence, to its budding days, as it dominated its territory as a trading village and a far outpost, to the days of urban glory. In some intriguing way, maps show St. Louis as a place, very broadly discerned, which has always been *there*, in local, national and historical consciousness.

John Neal Hoover
June 2014

Acknowledgments

It is with deep gratitude that I wish to thank friends and colleagues for help and support on this project, the scale of which called forth the best efforts of many individuals: at the St. Louis Mercantile Library: Julie Dunn-Morton, Curator of Art; Sean Visintainer, Curator of the Herman T. Pott Inland Waterways Historical Collections; Nicolas Fry, Curator of the John W. Barriger Railroad Historical Collections; Charles Brown, Head of the Reference Room; as well as Amanda Schneider, Andrea Miller, Rebecca Thorn and Robert Manley also from the staff of the Mercantile Library, who helped on everything from proof reading to framing and mounting the accompanying exhibition.

Emily Troxel Jaycox of the Missouri History Museum's Library, Robert Moore of the National Park Service, and Waller McGuire of the St. Louis Public Library, and Tom Serfass, Curataor of the Eric P. Newman Numistatic Education Society were extremely generous with advice for the exhibition and/or the facilitation of loans of objects from their institutions. Florence Jumonville of the University of New Orleans was very forthcoming with her advice and knowledge of the history of the Mississippi Valley. I am also grateful to Peter J. Kastor, Professor of History at Washington University in St. Louis, Brian Dunnigan, Clements Library, University of Michigan, and Steven Rowan, Professor of History at the University of Missouri–St. Louis, for the free and generous offering of their own knowledge and expertise on cartographical history. For the additional loans of Baron von Egloffstein's maps of St. Louis County and Bellefontaine Cemetery, I am indebted to Steve Kerber, Lovejoy Library, Southern Illinois University at Edwardsville, and to Nancy Ylvisaker, President, Bellefontaine Cemetery Association.

Patricia Archer, graphic designer and printing compositor of this catalogue for the exhibition and photgrapher August Jennewein merit special praise for seeing this complicated project through the press so successfully. The Board of Direction of the St. Louis Mercantile Library Association never flagged in offering support and aid to the promotion of this project as was the same with the Library's University of Missouri-St. Louis partners under Chancellor Tom George and Dean of Libraries, Christopher Dames.

For financial support for this project the Mercantile Library is abidingly grateful as well to the Orthwein Foundation, the Pershing Charitable Trust, BNSF Railway Foundation, and the Herman T. and Phenie R. Pott Foundation, and to Mr. Blackford F. "Beau" Brauer for their generosity and enthusiasm. Beau Brauer not only made generous gifts for the success of the project but offered many key design suggestions for its success as well as promoted the program tirelessly, making the entire experience a great pleasure to assemble and present to the St. Louis public. To all of these generous individuals and others too numerous to mention go the sincere thanks of the Director of the St. Louis Mercantile Library Association.

JNH

Introduction

Peter J. Kastor

There is something remarkable about the maps of early America. In an era when the limits of geographic knowledge were matched by the limits of printing technology, people somehow managed to produce a large number of highly detailed images of the North American continent. Their work is often captivating, occasionally beautiful, and always fascinating. Of course, these early maps presented fantasy as often as reality, but that is what makes them so revealing. Through words and pictures, maps demonstrated the knowledge and ignorance, the aspirations and fears, the possibilities and the dangers of the American experience.

Mapping St. Louis History is so compelling because it recaptures a world that is so elusive to us today. Satellite images, GIS data, and the computers that transmit this information throughout the global digital network now provide near-instantaneous access to the world's geography, both natural and man-made. Very quickly we have lost sight of a world that existed not so long ago, a world in which people rarely knew what lay over the horizon. The world of computerized mapping also serves as a reminder that form is often no less important than content. In the same way that geographic data is useless without the internet that transmits it or the computers that analyze it, so too was geographic knowledge in an earlier age dependent on the books and maps that circulated that knowledge to a world eager to learn about North America.

Nowhere was the power of mapping more evident than in the place that became the city of St. Louis. The story of St. Louis and the maps that told that story come together to reveal three interlocking perspectives on the past. First, they demonstrate the multi-national, multi-racial contest that gripped North America for centuries. Second, they help tell a story of North American cities, one in which the emerging metropolises of the continental interior both confirm but also challenge the more familiar story of cities of the East and West coasts. Third, they recapture a disappearing world that predated the computer and the internet, a world in which the printed page was an object of tremendous value because it was so difficult to produce.

Long before a trading outpost called St. Louis was founded in 1764, people had sought to map the region containing the confluence of the Mississippi and Missouri rivers. They did so because Indians and Europeans alike were scrambling for control of a region at the center of an imperial contest that eventually helped create the United States and transform North America.

For centuries, different Indian groups had sought to control the region connecting the Mississippi and Missouri rivers. They competed with each other for regional dominance, only to find their numbers decimated by the epidemic diseases that came with the Europeans. Those pandemics moved faster and farther than the Europeans who carried them, spreading death and dislocation throughout the Indian world. By the mid-seventeenth century, the Indians who remained in the mid-Mississippi Valley encountered not only a few scattered Europeans, but also a flood of Indian refugees who were themselves the survivors of wars and disease further East.

As the Indians sought to construct a new set of relationships in the continental interior, European empires jostled among themselves for control of the Mississippi River. The French were the first to do so in earnest, seeing in the Mississippi River a quick and direct route that would connect French settlements in Canada to the Gulf of Mexico, the Atlantic, and finally to Europe. With French leaders claiming the Mississippi as the eastern boundary of a vast colony of Louisiana, a variety of explorers, merchants, and priests sought to extend the French hold on Indian country with varying degrees of success.

Unable to convince French settlers to move to North America in large numbers, the French government relied on an alliance system between French colonial officials, Indians, and a small number of French merchants. By the mid-eighteenth century, the French had established a series of towns and trading outposts that reflected their broader imperial strategy.

One of those outposts, St. Louis, was founded in 1764. Although a visionary Frenchman—Pierre Laclède—brought the town into being and helped recruit its early French population, St. Louis was in many ways a reflection of Indian power. Indians permitted the French to build and maintain St. Louis because they believed the outpost would advance their own commercial interests. Thomas Hutchins' 1781 map, *Plan des Villiages de la Contree des Illinois et Partie de la Riviere de Mississipi*, shows how French outposts and Indian villages dotted the landscape of the mid-Mississippi valley.

St. Louis and the other French trading outposts stood in marked contrast to the settlements of the other major European players in North America: Great Britain and Spain.

To the west, Spain had struggled to extend its reach into what is now Texas and Mexico. Abandoning the vision of conquest that characterized their empires in Central and South America, the Spanish relied primarily on Catholic missions and military outposts to build influence with North American Indians. In 1763, France ceded most of its Louisiana colony to Spain. News of the cession did not reach the North American interior until after St. Louis was founded the following year. In the decades that followed, the Spanish always saw Louisiana as a buffer to protect their more valuable colonies to the southwest. A few

Spanish settlers and a handful of officials came to St. Louis, where French quite literally remained the *lingua franca*. Louisiana proved to be of so little value to Spain that the Spanish returned the colony to France in 1800.

To the east, the British had followed a very different imperial policy. Immigrants by the thousands were eager to leave the British Isles, establishing a European population base in eastern North America. Focusing on agriculture rather than trade, white settlers coveted Indian land. By the time the British colonies declared their independence in 1776, most Anglo-American settlers had abandoned the older systems of alliance, negotiation, and accommodation that the French and the Indians had developed in the West.

The Indian world of the Mississippi Valley and the Anglo-American world of the East collided in 1803, when France sold its colony of Louisiana to the United States. The news came as a surprise to American policymakers, who had sought to consolidate their control *east* of the Mississippi rather than rush to expand *west*. And in the years that followed, governing the newly acquired territories would be among the greatest domestic policymaking challenges facing the United States. American officials committed themselves to establishing opportunities for whites and preserving racial supremacy over African Americans. Meanwhile, in a final break from the practices first established by Indians and the French, the United States sought to extinguish Indian power and remove Indian villages.

The distinct but overlapping developments of imperial contest, commercial expansion, and white settlement had combined to fuel an elusive quest for geographic information. From the moment Europeans arrived in the New World, they sought to map out their discoveries and their territorial claims. But throughout the sixteenth, seventeenth, and eighteenth centuries, the continental interior remained a mystery.

The first maps in this exhibition powerfully demonstrate the extent and—more often—the limitations of European geographic knowledge.

They also show the bizarre guesses that Europeans were only too willing to put in print. Louis Armand, Baron de Lahontan, tried repeatedly to produce a map of North America. With its emphasis on rivers, his 1705 *Carte Generale De Canada* captures the French effort to build commercial networks that depended on rivers for transposition and communication. Meanwhile, Guillaume De l'Isle's landmark 1718 map, *Carte de la Louisiane et du Cours du Mississippi*, was among the first maps to emphasize the strategic value of the confluence of waterways in the mid-Mississippi valley. Maps like Lahontan and De L'Isle's would help convince French officials and French merchants to establish the outpost that became St. Louis.

These early maps were printed from metal plates produced by highly skilled engravers. Color had to be hand-drawn or hand-painted. As a result, maps were rare and expensive. But maps were more than elegant objects to satisfy the curiosity of the Enlightenment. They were policymaking tools that diplomats and governing officials relied upon to determine boundaries, to oversee settlement, and to judge the threats and challenges facing them. They were also windows to the fantasies and ambitions of the people seeking to shape the future of North America.

The maps in this exhibition from the seventeenth and eighteenth centuries chronicle the overlapping European territorial claims. Maps from the nineteenth century likewise show the United States as it expanded through the acquisition of new territory and the creation of new states. The story that Americans usually tell about westward expansion is often situated on a farm, or a ranch, or an open prairie. But the French history serves as a reminder that European settlement and conquest had an important urban dimension. Outposts, towns, and finally cities soon appeared throughout the North American landscape. St. Louis would exemplify both the history of urban development, as well as the challenges that came with it.

When the United States acquired Louisiana from France in 1803, St. Louis was home to approximately 2,000 people. White settlers soon descended on the land beyond the Mississippi River. Not only was visiting St. Louis a common experience for thousands of migrants hoping to establish their own farms further west, but supplying those migrants and selling what they produced became the business of a permanent population that sometimes grew faster than the city's resources could support. By 1810, St. Louis had gone from outpost to small town, and by 1850 it had transformed into a city in its own right. St. Louis announced to the rest of the world its arrival as a true metropolis in 1904, when the city hosted a celebration of the centennial of the Louisiana Purchase, an event now known as the 1904 World's Fair. Only four years earlier, the 1900 census had determined that St. Louis was the fourth most populace city in the United States.

Maps tell this story of urban growth. Lewis Beck's *Plan of St. Louis* from 1822 is among the earliest representations of the city in any medium. That he chose to include it in his *Gazeteer of Illinois and Missouri* is no less important. Beck knew that Americans not only wanted to *read* about the new settlements in the West; they wanted to *see* them as well. Compare the small town of Beck's map to the growing city of Julius Hutawa's 1851 map. In barely three decades, St. Louis had been transformed. But Hutawa's map, with its clear lines and nicely divided wards, belies just how chaotic that growth had become. This was a crowded, messy, confusing city filled with newcomers. Although the federal government had forced most Indians from Missouri in the 1820s and '30s and the old French population had become a distinct minority, St. Louis remained a multiracial, multi-ethnic city. White residents lived alongside African-Americans, both enslaved and free. St. Louis may have been distant from the Gulf of Mexico or the Atlantic, but thousands of European immigrants chose the city as their destination.

Throughout the mid-nineteenth century, land developers and railroad companies engaged in a mad scramble throughout the West, creating unpredictable land ownership and convulsive land values. Even as railroads eclipsed riverboats, the docks along Mississippi River remained flooded with vessels of all kinds. Indeed, it was in an effort to control the unpredictable waters of the Mississippi that the U.S. Army

Corps of Engineers dispatched one of its most talented young officers, Lieutenant Robert E. Lee, to survey the river. Lee's 1837 map of the river captures St. Louis in an era of transformation.

All of these changes combined to make St. Louis very much like the other growing cities of the United States. It shared more in common with distant locales like Philadelphia, Baltimore, or Charleston than it did with the nearby farm settlements of eastern Missouri. Nor was St. Louis unique. The growth of New Orleans had kept pace with St. Louis. Anglo-Americans towns like Cincinnati, Louisville, and Nashville amazed outside observers with the speed of their growth. The most remarkable success story was Chicago, which began life as a minor French trading outpost located on the overland portage between the Illinois River and Lake Michigan. By 1860, Chicago had eclipsed even St. Louis.

As Chicago grew, St. Louisans held onto the belief that St. Louis was the logical center of gravity in a country that was drifting inexorably west. That fantasy took visual form in L. U. Reavis' *Map Illustrative of the continental Argument in Favor of St. Louis Becoming the Future Great City of the World*. Unrealistic in so many ways, Reavis' map nonetheless captured both the optimism of many St. Louisans, and the relentless entrepreneurialism at work in selling the city to the rest of the nation. The fact that Reavis used a map to make the case for St. Louis' greatness made sense as well, since he appropriated a long tradition of using maps to tell big stories.

As western cities like St. Louis continued to grow, so too did the number of maps and books that described them. And this was a marvel in its own right.

When the United States acquired Louisiana, there was no printing industry in St. Louis. Barely a half-century later St. Louis was home to a growing community of printers who produced all range of material for the growing St. Louis marketplace. St. Louisans consumed material produced locally, nationally, and around the world. The St. Louis Mercantile Library, which is hosting this exhibition, was itself a product of this boom in publishing and readership. Founded in 1846, the library showcased local publishing even as it purchased material produced throughout the Atlantic world.

Not only were westerners creating their own publishing capacity, but they could circulate increasingly accurate and detailed geographic information. After all, European printers may have been able to produce exquisite maps centuries earlier, but those maps were most remarkable for the *absence* of accurate details about the North American interior and the *abundance* of conjecture and outright fabrication. This state of affairs underwent a complete transformation in little more than a century. From the mid-eighteenth century through the late-nineteenth century, European explorers and surveyors set out to map North American in its entirety. To do so, they relied extensively on the support and the knowledge of Indians. In the end, that knowledge would contribute to the Indians' undoing. Geographic knowledge was a vital component to the American conquest of North America, one that resulted in death and dislocation for native peoples.

These early printers struggled for survival in an industry marked by high overhead, dangerously narrow profit margins, and the constant threat of bankruptcy. The maps in this collection are not just a chronicle of geographic knowledge or imperial contest or urban growth, but a story of publishing itself. The maps in his exhibition from the 1810s and '20s reveal a publishing industry in transition. Printers in the eastern United States had begun to displace their European counterparts in producing maps of North America. These American printers had the latest word in geographic knowledge, and their shops included the first generation of well-trained, highly skilled cartographic engravers. Meanwhile, a nascent printing industry was taking form in the West. Initially limited to producing travel guides and similar written descriptions of places like St. Louis, by the Civil War St. Louis possessed a local community of printers and engravers who could produce detailed and accurate maps of the city.

The intersection of publishing, territorial conquest, and western exploration is abundantly clear in a series of maps from the early 1800s. While French publishers like Francois Marie Perrin Du Lac were still producing important maps in 1805, their work coincided with western expeditions under men like Lewis and Clark or Zebulon Pike. Those expeditions produced their own books and maps that Europeans began to emulate in their own work.

By the late nineteenth century, American-made maps were once again showing a continent in transformation. The United States had successfully completed its plan to extinguish Indian sovereignty on a continental scale, relegating tribes to government-chosen reservations. Meanwhile, cities like St. Louis were the centers of an industrialized economy.

Maps would be no less important in the twentieth century, but they were increasingly easy to come by in a way that would have been the envy of earlier generations. The same industrial growth that had fueled the rise of St. Louis in the nineteenth century made it increasingly easy for American publishers to generate maps that were highly detailed, inexpensive, and widely distributed. Consider the products of Rand McNally, which came to dominate the American map industry, and which produced several maps that appear in this exhibition. Rand McNally's 1884 *New Sectional Map of Missouri* was a typical example of the emerging field of modern map publishing. Forty years later, Rand McNally was capitalizing on the growth of the automobile industry to produce the street maps of St. Louis and road maps of Missouri that would guide generations of Americans.

These late-nineteenth and early twentieth century maps were printed on paper made from wood pulp and were produced on steam-powered presses. They were a far cry from the hand-pressed cotton pages that had been the norm for generations. Yet if wood pulp was cheap and abundant, it was also more brittle than the older cloth paper. So if the earliest materials in this exhibition were scarce, often inaccurate, and always expensive, they actually were more durable than their more modern counterparts. Indeed, maps have continued to become more ephemeral even as they have become more accurate. In our own age of computer-generated maps, the visual image of the landscape often lasts only as long as the latest set of data or the current session on a Website. Yet the quest for geographic data remains, as does the artistry of representing that data in words and pictures.

Table of Contents

Part One:

[Fig. a]

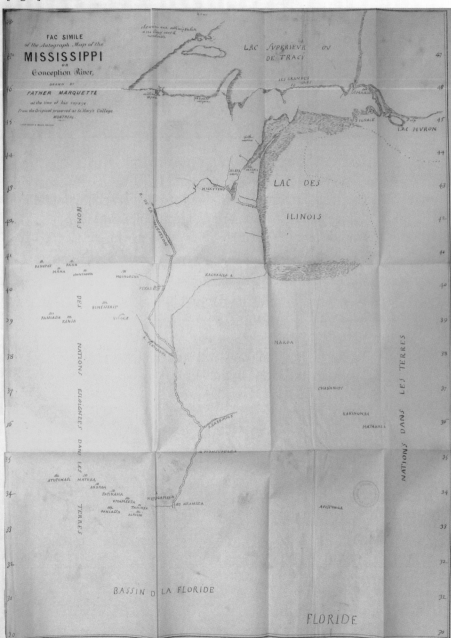

St. Louis was on maps at the headwaters of the growing realization of empire by the French and Spanish long before it was an actual place and these maps reveal the river confluence's future strategic importance at the heart of a continental empire. Father Marquette's early manuscript map was a prophetic document. **[Fig. a]**. Later this awareness of the western gateway which St. Louis was to become for a new American nation helped fuel Manifest Destiny. Look closely at these old maps however, in terms of settlement. Politics aside, it seems miraculous St. Louis does not have an earlier founding date when given the excellent prospects for any city at the confluence of the great rivers in the center of a vast region. Oftentimes "mines" are listed; minuscule dots mark temporary, at least, settlements. Native American tribes yield their names to tributaries and small villages nearby; Cahokia and Fort Chartres are always nearby and old forts and posts have a phantom-like quality appearing and disappearing with regularity on these charts. It was an open secret, perhaps this land, ripe for settlement but not yet established with any organizational aspect towards the future.

1   Thomas Gage. Untitled map from ***A New Survey of the West-Indias: or, the English American his Travail by Sea and Land: Containing a Journal of Three Thousand and Three Hundred Miles within the Main land of America***. London: E. Cotes, 1655. **[1]**

Gage wrote one of the most important English travel books on America in the 17th century, exciting the English with envy—never a difficult thing to do in those days—on the wealth and the relative defenselessness of the Spanish in North America, laying out a concrete plan for domination of the continent. This map gives an idea of the paucity of specific European knowledge of the interior of North America and especially Louisiana on the eve of concerted effort by the French to explore and colonize the region. Yet, even here one sees the great, beckoning mystery of a central river, the unnamed Mississippi, nearly connecting with a huge outstretched arm of the St. Lawrence, nothing shown as yet of the Great Lakes or the elusive northwest of the vast continent.

2 Jacques Marquette. Map accompanying text of *Ontdekking va eenige landen en volkeren, in 't noorder-gedeelte van America door P. Marquette en Joliet; geddan in het jaar 1673.* Leyden: Peter Vander Aa, 1707. **[2]** and **[Fig. a]** : *a meeting with natives in a Mississippi Valley village.*

An early printing of Marquette and Joliet's travels in the Mississippi valley providing some of the first detailed maps and images of the region.

[Fig. a]

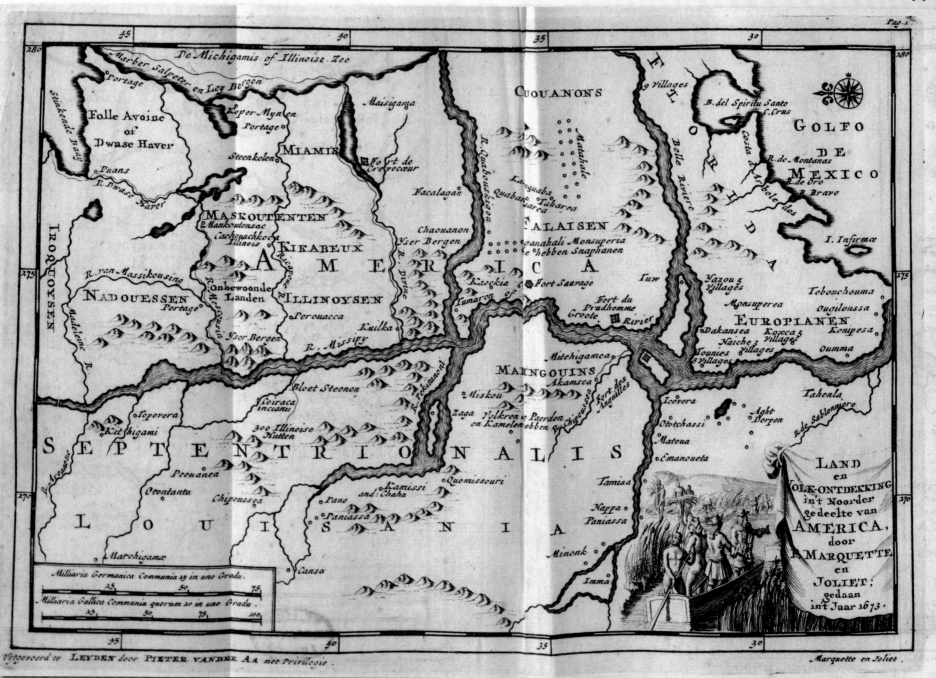

De Michigamis of Illinoise Zee

CUOUANONS

GOLFO DE MEXICO

IROQUOYSEN

AMERICA

SEPTENTRIONALIS

LOUISANIA

LAND en VOLK-ONTDEKKING in't Noorder gedeelte van AMERICA, door P. MARQUETTE en JOLIET; gedaan in't Jaar 1673.

Milliaria Germanica Communia 15 in uno Gradu.

Milliaria Gallica Communia quorum 20 in uno Gradu.

Uitgevoerd te LEYDEN door PIETER VANDER AA met Privilegie.

Marquette en Joliet.

3 Louis Hennepin. Selected maps accompanying *Beschryving van Louisania: Nieuwelijks ontdekt ten Zuid-Westen van Nieuw-Vrankryk, Door order van den Konig.* [3a] Amsterdam: Jan ten Hoorn, 1688. With Hennepin's *Nouveau voyage d'un pais plus grand que l'Europe: avec les reflections des enterprises de Sieur de l'Salle, sur les mines de St. Barbe, &c.* Utrecht: Antoine Schouten, 1698. [3b]. [Fig. a]: *"Buffalo"*; [Fig. b]: *"Native in landscape"*; [Fig. c]: *frontispiece with a traveler, (Hennepin?) with his map.*

[Fig. a]

Hennepin was one of the first explorers to use the term and develop the concept of a place called "Louisiana." He was the great popularizer of the world of New France, after years of travel and exploration. His works reflected an age of marketing the natural resources of the New World. Hennepin accompanied La Salle to the Illinois River in 1679, at that point splitting off, ascending the Mississippi and seeing for the first time as a white man a river that the Indians reverenced as much as any seventeenth century priest did his own Christianity. He penetrated farther into the interior of the continent than any explorer before him, seeing not only the Mississippi but Niagara Falls and the abundance of flora and fauna in the vast Illinois country of the French.

[Fig. b]

[Fig. c]

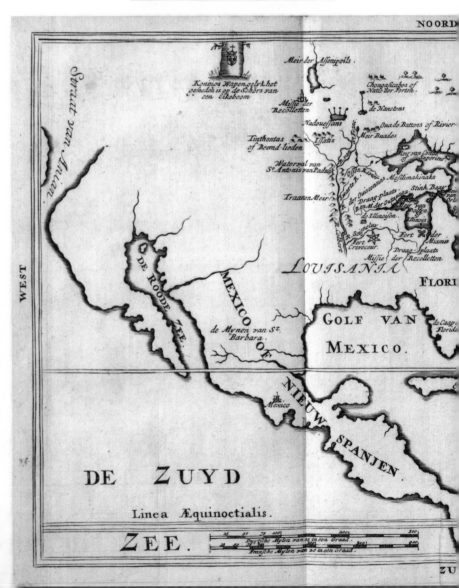

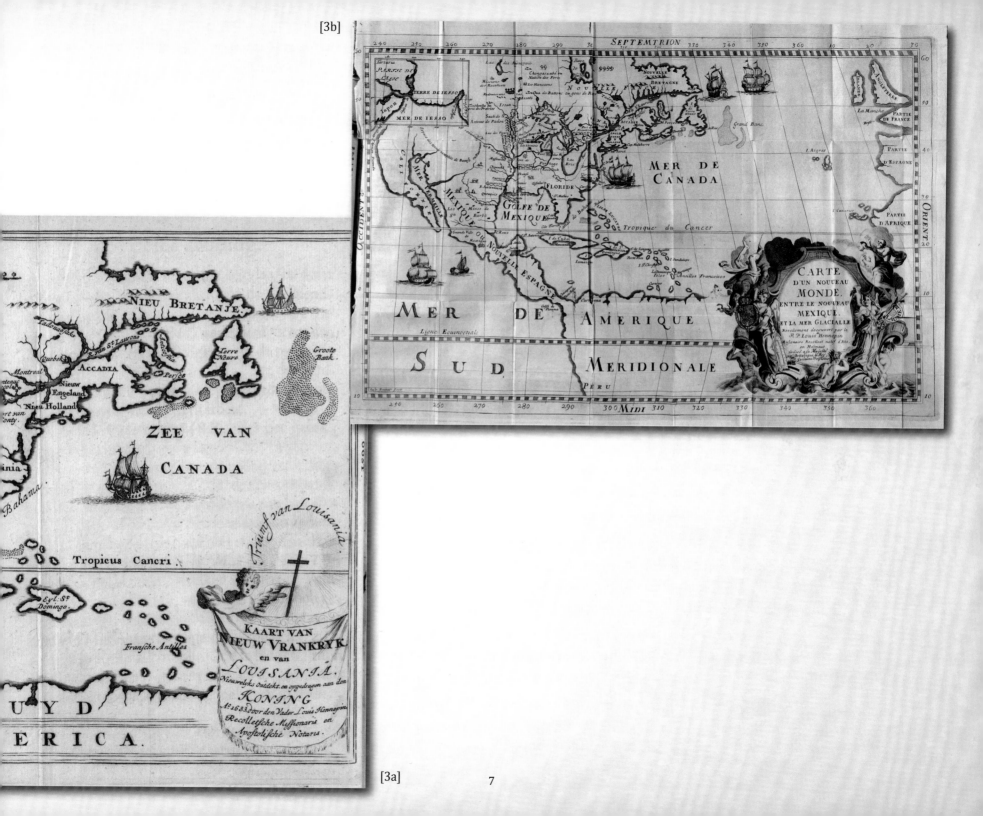

[3b]

[3a]

4 Louis Armand, Baron de Lahontan. *"Carte generale de Canada"* a sprawling map opening *Voyages dans l'Amerique Septentrionale qui contiennent une Relation des differens Peuples qui y habitent: la nature de leur Gouvernement; leur Commerce, leur Coutumes, leur Religion et leur maniere de faire la Guerre.* Amsterdam: Francois l'Honere. 1705 **[4]**. **[Fig. a]**: *"French habitation"*; **[Fig. b]**: *"Natives"*.

A soldier who travelled extensively through the early military defenses of New France, Lahontan related a very early picture of the western lands, one of the most comprehensive to his time and his maps of the Great Lakes and the Upper Mississippi are some of the first to show the Missouri-Mississippi river confluence. Lahontan was an especially valuable correspondent on the state of the native peoples of the French colonial lands.

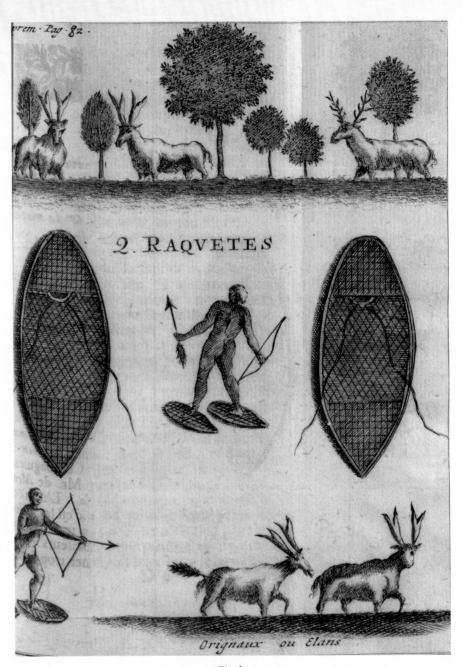

Fig. b

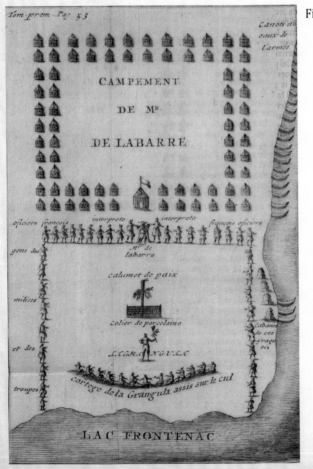

Fig. a

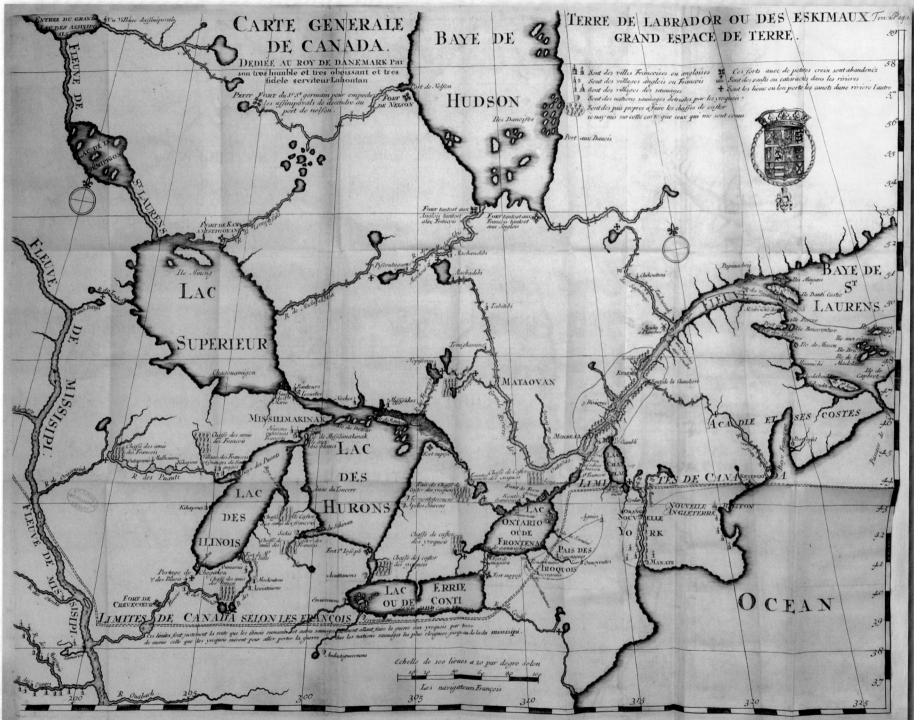

4

CARTE GENERALE DE CANADA.

DEDIEE AU ROY DE DANEMARK Par son tres humble et tres obeissant et tres fidele serviteur Lahontan.

TERRE DE LABRADOR OU DES ESKIMAUX Tem.2 Pag.1
GRAND ESPACE DE TERRE.

BAYE DE HUDSON

BAYE DE St LAURENS

FLEUVE DE St LAURENS

LAC SUPERIEUR

LAC DES HURONS

LAC DES ILINOIS

FLEUVE DE MISSISIPI

LAC ONTARIO OU DE FRONTENAC

LAC ERRIE OU DE CONTI

ACADIE ET SES COSTES

NOUVELLE ANGLETERRE

NOUVELLE YORK

PAIS DES IROQUOIS

OCEAN

LIMITES DE CANADA SELON LES FRANCOIS

Echelle de 100 lieues a 20 par degré selon

Les navigateurs François

9

5 Henri Joutel. Untitled map of New France from *Journal historique du dernier voyage que feu M. de la Sale fit dans le Golfe de Mexique trouver l'embouchere, & le cours de la Riviere de Missicipi, nommee a present de Saint Louis, qui traverse la Louisiane.*
Paris: Estienne Robinot, 1713. **[5]**

This is the first map reporting the last two expeditions of La Salle which related La Salle's celebrated Mississippi exploration and became the first accurate delineation of the river system of the vast French empire. In spite of the hardships of Joutel in making his way back to Canada after the tragic death of La Salle and the breakup of the ill-fated expedition, he produced a fine account and one of the best maps to his time of the Mississippi River. Personal copy of Auguste Chouteau, donated to the St. Louis Mercantile Library Association.

5

Renvoy des Lettres.

A...Bouche d'une petite Riviere située aux 28.º 17. Lat.
Nord et 271.º de Longitude où s'est fait le premier débarquement de l'Auteur.
B...Bouche d'un bras de la susdite Riviere qui rend dans la Baye de S.ᵗ Loüis, et forme un islet à la pointe duquel vers l'entrée de la Baye a été fait la premiere Habitation.
C...Riviere inconnuë.
D...Riviere aux Boeufs, sur le bord de la quelle on a fait une seconde Habitation, au dessus de la quelle ladite R. se sépare en 2. bras.
E...Riviere aux Cannes, ainsi apellée depuis son Embouchure jusqu'à la fourche qui la sépare en 2. bras, dont celui qui est à droit est apelé R. Mignone, acause des amours d'un nommé le S.ᵗ Barbier Lieutenant, et se répare encore au dessus en trois autres; celui qui est à gauche de la premiere fourche s'apelle Princesse acause de la même raison.
F...Riviere de la Sablonniere.
G...Riviere de Hiems dont la chute est inconnuë.
H...Riviere Latier dont la chute est inconnuë.
I...Grande Riv. apellée la Maligne.
K...Riviere d'Esvre, dont la chute est inconnuë.
L...Riviere aux Canots, dont la chute est inconnuë.
M...Riviere sans nom, dont la chute est inconnuë.
N...Premiere Riviere assez belle de la Nation des Cenis, dont la chute est inconnuë.
O...Autre Riviere qui passe par le Village des Cenis, dont la chute est inconnuë.
P...Seconde Habitation de laquelle nous sommes partis avec Monsieur de la Salle, et avons traversé toutes les Rivieres cy-dessus dénommées, avec des Lettres, par le chemin marqué par des points de cette sorte....................pour arriver à la Riviere des Acanseas à l'endroit où elle se Fourche, où nous trouvasmes une Maison marquée R. habitée de deux François, auquel lieu nous étant embarquez, nous avons baisé jusqu'au Fleuve Missisipi, que nous avons ensuite remonté jusqu'à la Riviere des Illinois.
Nota qu'en cette année 1712. la Riviere Missisipi a changé de nom, et qu'elle s'apelle R. de S.ᵗ Loüis.
Q...Boeuf du pays dont le poil est long et fin côme la Soye. Il y en a une infinité.
R...Le fameux Saut de Niagara, où la R. de S.ᵗ Laurent tombe de plus de 100. Toises de haut.

6 Johann Baptist Homann. *Amplissimae regionis Mississipi seu provinciae Ludovicianae a R.P. Ludovico Hennepin Frencise Miss. In America Septemtrionali.* (Reprinted from the Homann 1716 world atlas and most likely appearing in Atlas Geographicus Major Norimbergae Homannianis Heredibus. Nuremberg: J. B. Homann, 1763, a time of renewed interest in Old World colonial land claims at the close of the French and Indian War.) **[6a]**

This great map is a cartographic *masterwork*, based on Jesuit Father Louis Hennepin's wanderings and narratives of La Salle's explorations, published in 1697 (see Item **[3]**), and De l'Isle's seminal maps (see Item **[7]**). Hennepin is depicted in the inset of the upper left corner, the first European to view Niagara Falls, as well as St. Anthony Falls, the only natural waterfall on the Mississippi besides smaller, foaming cataracts of the upper Mississippi. The source of the Mississippi is shown "based on the reports of Indians." Homann was a distinguished German cartographer, who followed Hennepin and later French mapmakers in labelling the land west of the Appalachians as it came to be known, *Louisiane*, thus helping to incur the wrath of both England and Spain in the mad and avaricious rush for territory in North America. On this map New Orleans is situated on the wrong side of the Mississippi. Mines, ruins and old forts are shown in the St. Louis area and the Illinois region. With Homann's contemporary map *Regni Mexicani seu Novae Hispaniae, Ludovicianae, N. Angliae etc.*, an interesting chart showing Louisiana demarcated from the Illinois country. On this map is shown much better knowledge of the Osage, the Missouri and other tribes, the traditional French trading partners of the St. Louis region **[6b]**.

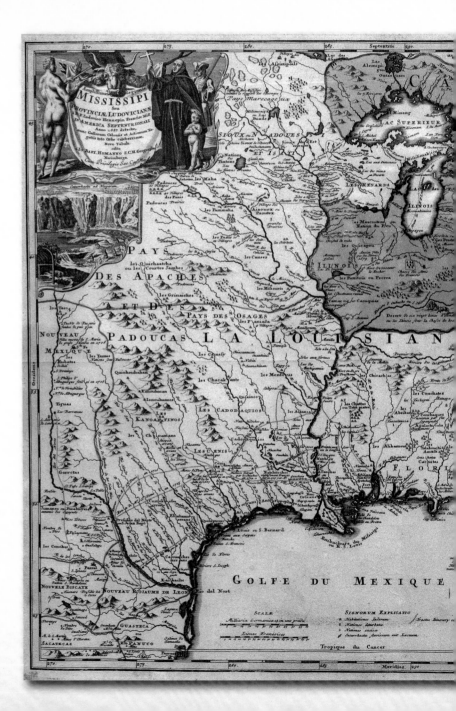

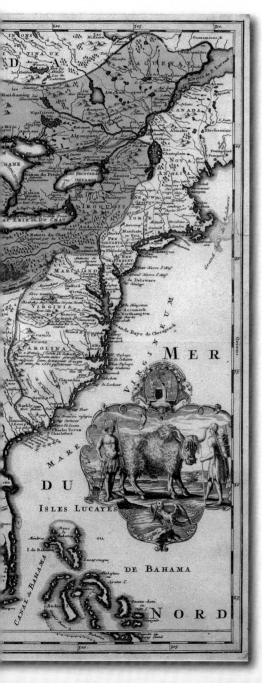

7 Guillaume De l'Isle *Carte de la Louisiane et du Cours du Mississippi (from Atlas Nouveau Contenant Toutes Les Parties du Monde*. Paris, 1718; with two other maps by de l'Isle printed by his subsequent publisher, Amsterdam: Covens and Mortier, 1742. [7]

Guillaume De l'Isle's "Map of Louisiana and the Mississippi River" is one of the most famous maps in American history, what cartographers call, because of its accuracy and eloquence, a "mother map," a map in this case that spurred great imitation, innovation, and political thought. The map was originally published in 1718, the year this mapmaker was appointed Chief Geographer to the King (Louis XIV). This map of New France was used as a reference point for another half century and considered the most authoritative of the Mississippi Valley. It tracked the expeditions of De Soto, de Tonty and Louis de St. Denis. No wonder it is usually found in multiple copies in all the major libraries of the St. Louis region. Accompanying the mother map are other works of early geo-politics worked up by De l'Isle and presented by his Amsterdam publishers—each showing the French lands in the context of a still relatively unexplored and unverified northwestern continent. **[Fig. a]**: *western hemisphere*; **[Fig. b]**: *both hemispheres*. Yet De l'Isle's importance for the St. Louis region is inarguable. His map of Louisiana is informed of the best authorities to his time. It is the first map to correct the position of the mouth of the Mississippi, and locate it accurately. A magisterial contribution to subsequent mapmaking is De l'Isle's correct depiction and alignment of the Mississippi River and the accurate positioning of the Mississippi Valley as a whole.

[Fig. a]

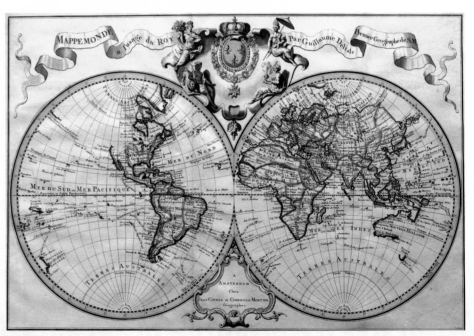

[Fig. b]

7

CARTE DE LA LOUISIANE ET DU COURS DU MISSISSIPI Dressée sur un grand nombre de Memoires entrautres sur ceux de Mr le Maire Par Guillme Delisle de l'Academie Rle des Sciences

GOLFE DU MEXIQUE

MER DU NORD

A PARIS
Chez l'Auteur le Sr Delisle
sur le Quay de l'Horloge
avec Privilege du Roy Juin 1718

Explication des Marques

CARTE PARTICULIERE DES EMBOUCHURES DE LA RIVIE S. LOUIS ET DE LA MOBILE

8

John Senex. *A Map of Louisiana and of the River Mississippi.*
(ca. 1719, From Senex's *A New General Atlas.* London: Browne,
Taylor, et al, 1721). **[8]**

[Fig. a]

Senex, an astronomer and geologist, became a popular map maker of world maps in miniature, early pocket sized maps, and almanac maps. For this chart, an accurate map for the English speaking world for its time, he borrowed heavily from the De l'Isle map (see Item **[7]**). His work did not extend to duplicating French claims to Carolina, which would be reinforced by the important English map by Coxe (Item **[10]**) which reduced all of French Louisiana to an English "Carolana" in fact. Ironically this map is dedicated to John Law, whose infamous "Mississippi Bubble" inflated stock scheme for the region of the Mississippi River, proved the financial ruin of many Europeans of the early eighteenth century. **[Fig. a]** shows a caricature from the Bubble scheme (collected in an acerbic set of tracts from 1720 and **[Fig. b]** shows an accurate account in German of the Louisiana of the day of the bubble scheme—the year it burst in fact. This broadside shows the De l'Isle/Senex contribution—a fine map glowingly depicting the region for economic gain and investment. **[Fig. c]** is a contemporary map of the river system from the Dutch edition of Law's own description of Louisiana's great prospects. The Mississippi Bubble of the early 17th century can be seen here to have put the St. Louis region "on the map" so to speak. It was immensely important in creating awareness of the faraway region, a remote wilderness. The broadside map and the accompanying text, published anonymously in Nuremberg in 1720, give a more-or-less factual presentation for the popular European mind at this time of what would become in time, a valley of many large and prosperous cities such as St. Louis, but as economic bubbles seem always to do, this one burst generations before its claims met true potential.

[Fig. c]

[Fig. b]

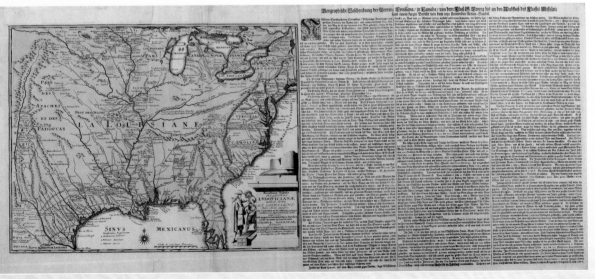

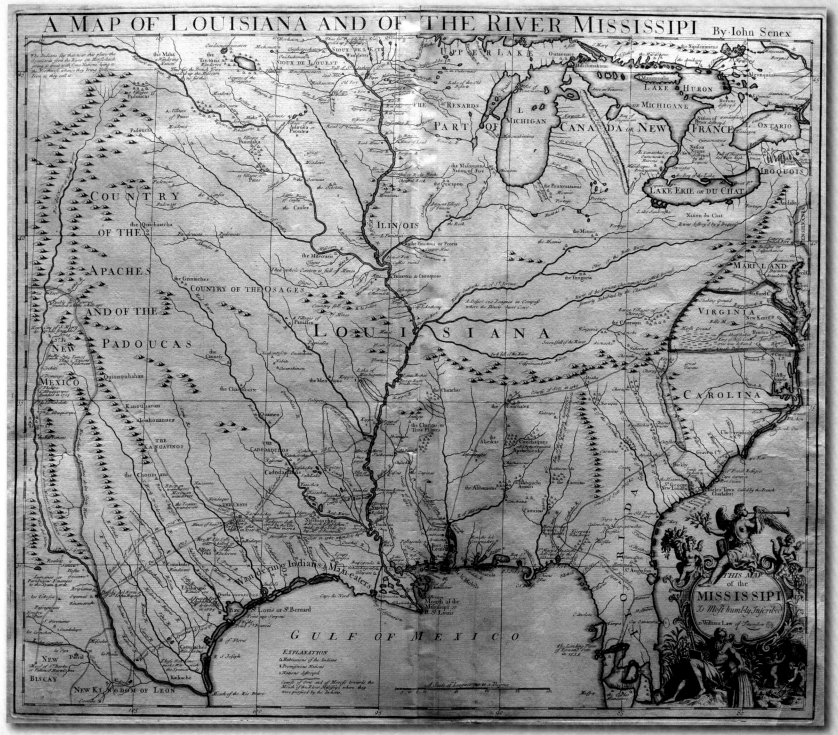

A MAP OF LOUISIANA AND OF THE RIVER MISSISSIPI
By Iohn Senex

9

Herman Moll. *A New Map of the North Parts of America Claimed by France Under the Names of Louisiana, Mississippi, Canada and New France with the Adjoining Territories of England and Spain.* London: H. Moll and John King, 1720. **[9]**

Moll, of Dutch or German origin, became along with Senex, one of England's most prominent mapmakers, creating highly distinctive and elegant representations as his 1720 map of America. As did his contemporary, John Senex (see Item **[8]**), Moll relied on De l'Isle's map for charting the Mississippi accurately. Moll was especially useful for his representation of locations of native tribes, yet, like many English cartographers of his day, adamantly stuck to the idea of California as an island—Senex was the same in this folly—but so much more was already known about the relatively unpopulated upper Mississippi and St. Louis at this time, a generation before settlement by Laclède and the Chouteaus.

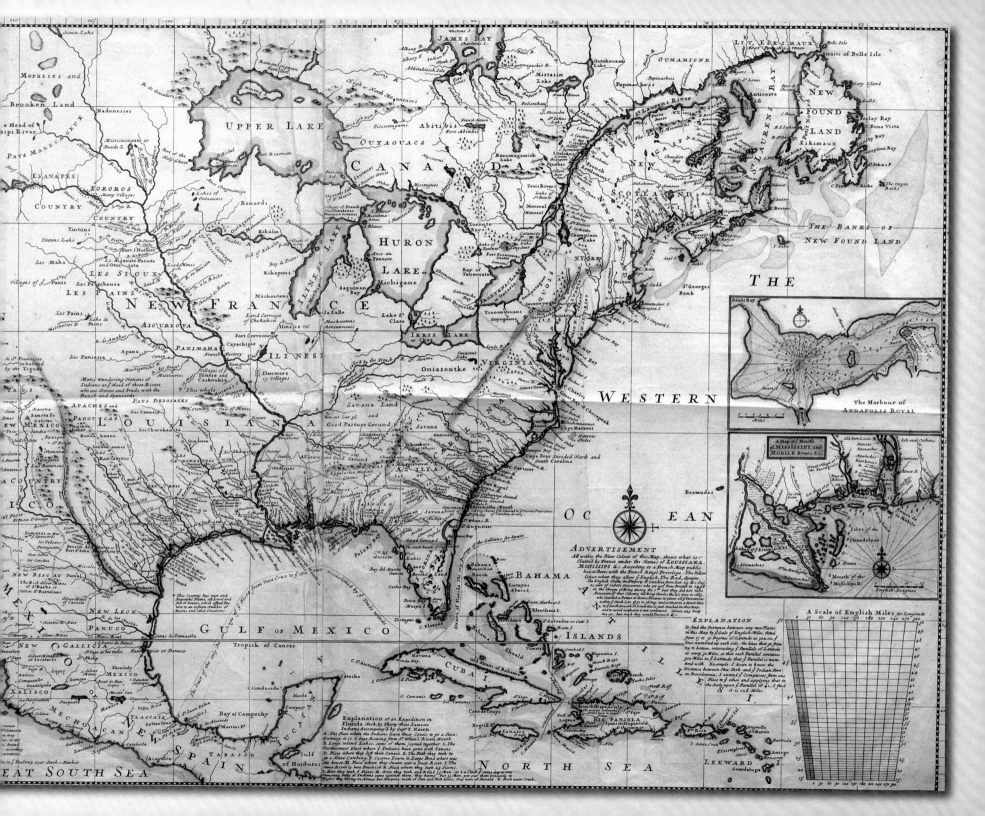

10 Daniel Coxe. *A Map of the Carolana and of the River Meschacebe.* (From *A Description of the English Province of Carolana by the Spaniards call'd Florida, and by the French Louisiane. Also of the Great and Famous River Meschacebe.*) London: Couse, 1722. **[10]**

An early 19th century copy in the Mercantile Library's John Mason Peck Collection of this, the first British exploration of the Mississippi Valley and the first English account of French Louisiana. The whole of the territory this map comprises was actually claimed by the father of Daniel Coxe, the author, as the would-be proprietor of the area under the Crown. The author lived in the region for many years and explored its fullest extent.

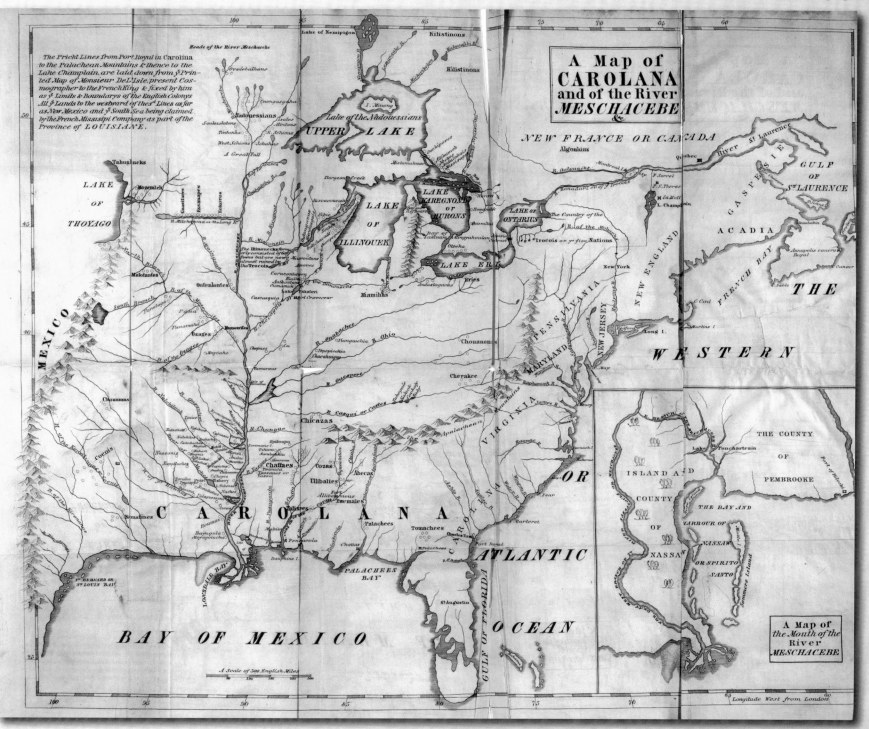

10

A Map of CAROLANA and of the River MESCHACEBE &c

The Prickt Lines from Port Royal in Carolina to the Palachean Mountains & thence to the Lake Champlain, are laid down from ye Printed Map of Monsieur DeL'Isle, present Cosmographer to the French King & fixed by him as ye Limits & Boundarys of the English Colonys. All ye Lands to the westward of these Lines as far as New Mexico and ye South Sea being claimed by the French Missisipi Company as part of the Province of LOUISIANE.

A Scale of 500 English Miles

A Map of the Mouth of the River MESCHACEBE

11 Henry Popple. ***Nouvelle Carte Particuliere de l'Amerique, ou sont Exactement Marquees, une Partie de la Bay d'Hudson, le Pays des Kilistonons, la Source de la Grand Riviere de Mississipi, le Pays des Illinois &c.*** Amsterdam: Covens and Mortier, 1741. **[11]**

Popple was an associate of astronomer and mathematician, Edmund Halley, and the advertisement in the inset cartouche for this map stresses that friendship in an endorsement for the map's accuracy, depicting fields, forts, towns, rivers, bogs, forests, all from St. Louis' future area, well mapped, showing the Missouri River in detailed positioning, also the Meramec River, Cahokia and Kaskaskia to the projected source of the Mississippi, making the most detailed English attempt to map the reaches of the upper Mississippi to its time.

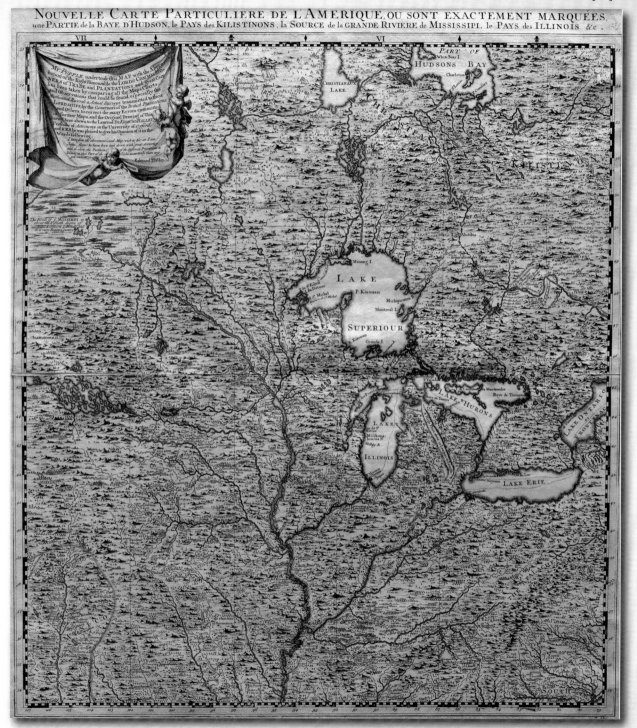

11

12 Pierre Francois Xavier de Charlevoix. *Carte de la Louisiane cours du Mississipi et Pays Voisins* (From *Histoire et Description generale de la Nouvelle France avec le Journal historique d'un voyage fait par ordre du Roi dans L'Amerique Septentrionale*). Paris: Noyon fils, 1744. **[12]**

With numerous botanical illustrations and splendid maps by hydrographer, Jacques-Nicholas Bellin, Charlevoix represents a culmination in the middle of the eighteenth century of what the French knew, or thought they knew, about North America and its rivers and varied lands drained by them. He was sent to North America to find a route to the Pacific and through years of travel and study recommended doing this by the ascent of the Missouri River or through the establishment of posts along traditional native trading routes in Canada, through strategic stepping stones. Charlevoix and Bellin set out to prove that the Missouri and the Mississippi had basically the same headwaters, and the maps in these volumes reflect that thinking in the supposed nearness of the sources of both rivers. The Great Lakes through a vast system not only were connected to the Atlantic but to the Pacific as well. The works of the French explorers and cartographers heavily interested Thomas Jefferson. Charlevoix considered the confluence of the Missouri and Mississippi Rivers the finest in the world.

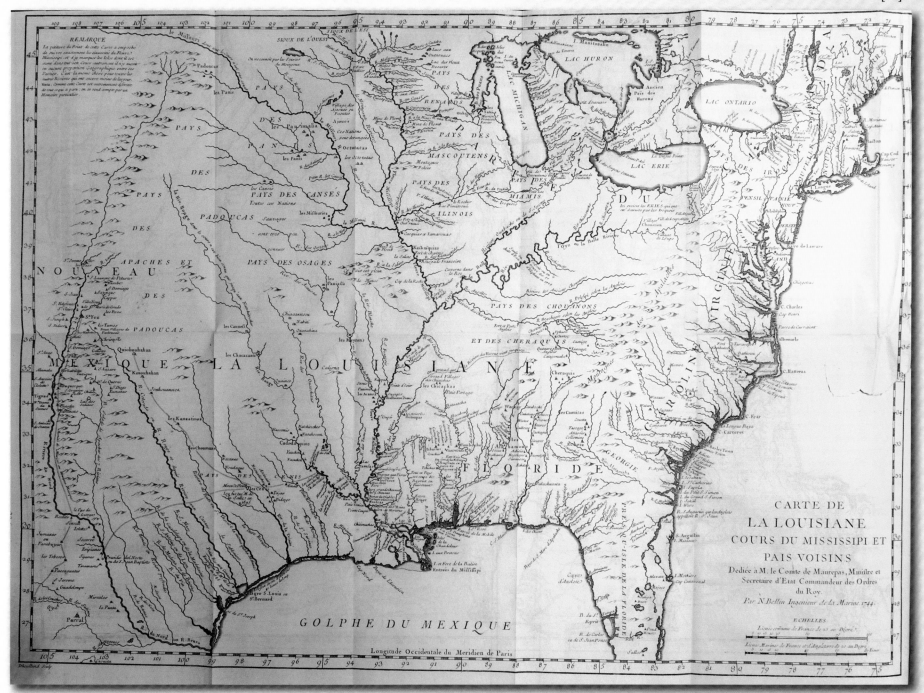

12

13

Thomas Kitchen. *A New and Accurate Map of the British Dominions in America according to the Treaty of 1763 Divided into the several Provinces and Jurisdictions Projected upon the Best Authorities, and Astronomical Observations.* From John Knox. *An Historical Journal of the Campaigns in North America for the Years 1757, 1759, and 1760.* London: Johnston and Dodsley, 1697. **[13]**

The map of North America at the time of the founding of St. Louis, with the 1776 extremely accurate map by Jean Baptiste Bourguignon D'Anville, *Carte General du Canada, de la Louisiane, de la Floride, de la Caroline, de la Virginie, de la Nouvelle Angleterre &c.* **[Fig. a]**; and **[Fig. b]**: Peter Bell's 1772 Map of the *British Dominions in North America* (from *The History of the British Dominions in North America. London: Strahan and Becket, 1773;* all of these maps reflecting a reordering of empires and the movement of settlers as a result of colonial warfare.

[Fig. b]

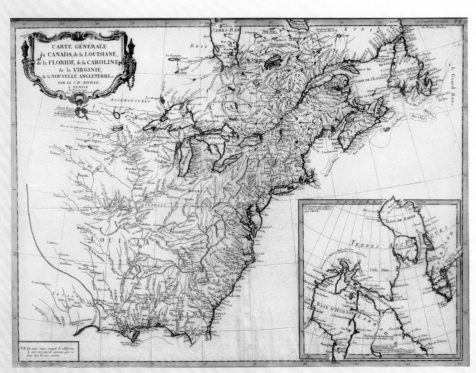

[Fig. a]

14 John Ross. *Course of the River Mississipi, from the Balise to Fort Chartres; Taken on an Expedition to the Illinois, in the latter end of the Year 1765.* (From: Thomas Jefferys. *The American Atlas.* London: Robert Sayer, 1778.) **[14]**

Based on surveys conducted only a few years after the Treaty of Paris ceded lands east of the Mississippi to England, Lieutenant Ross' detailed map was a significant advance over such distinguished French cartographers as D'Anville. On a scale like few others for the length of river depicted, the Ross map was widely held to be the most reliable map of the river produced in the 18th century—it clearly evidences the Mississippi Valley's growing social, political, commercial and agricultural significance. Ross respected the east side boundary of British occupation for observation purposes—hence familiar villages are noted but not the new up and coming settlement of St. Louis, with which British soldiers were clearly aware as the French were renewing their hold on the west bank of the River after their vast empire was torn in two. Jefferys also published a short description of upper Louisiana in *The Natural and Civil History of the French Dominions of North and South America* in 1760 which, on the eve of St. Louis' founding, could have used Ross' field notes. **[Fig. a]**.

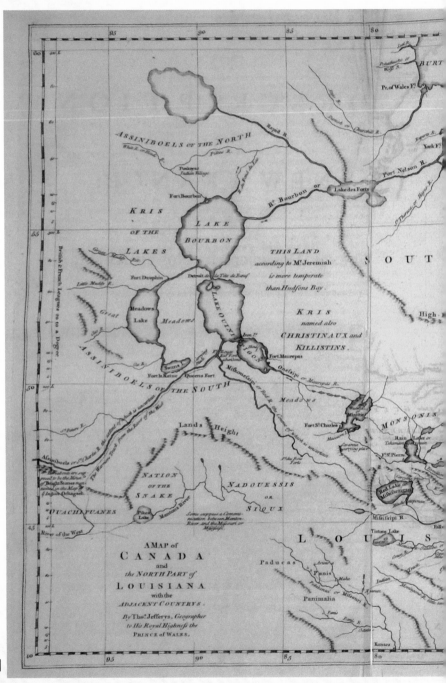

[Fig. a]

28

14

15 Philip Pittman. ***Draught of the River Mississippi from the Balise up to Fort Chartres.*** (From *The Present State of the European Settlements on the Missisippi with a Geographical Description of that River Illustrated by Plans and Draughts.*) London: J. Nourse, 1770. **[15]**

This is the most important description of old and new settlements along the Mississippi River Valley in English in the 18th century by a soldier who volunteered to bring new knowledge to the British command in North America concerning Louisiana, all readers having to the time of publication of this new book depended far too long on out of date sources. Pittman himself had noted that "Louisiana is no longer the same as in the time of Pere Henepin, and all other authors that I have read on this subject rather abound with Indian stories and talks, than with useful information". He was in St. Louis two years after its establishment, and observed its progress directly. He mapped the region thoroughly for his government as Ross had done, to Fort Chartres.

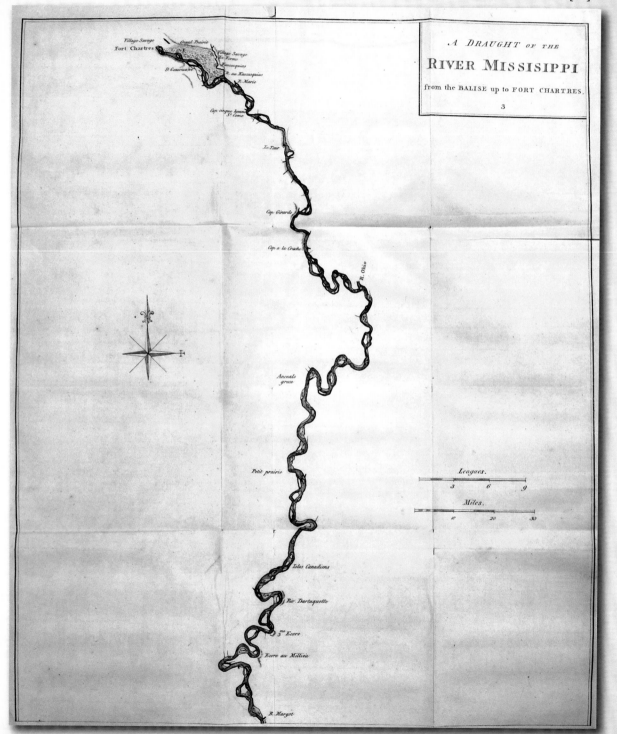

15

A DRAUGHT OF THE

RIVER MISSISIPPI

from the BALISE up to FORT CHARTRES.

3

16

Thomas Hutchins. ***Plan des Villiages de la Contree des Illinois et Partie de la Riviere de Mississipi.*** (From *Description Topographique de la Virginie, de la Pennsylvanie, du Maryland e de la Caroline Septentrionale.*) Paris: Chez le Rouge, Geographe, rue des Grands-Augustins, 1781) **[16a]** and *"A New Map of the Western Parts of Virginia, Pennsylvania, Maryland, and North Carolina Comprehending River Ohio and all the Rivers which fall into it; Part of the River Mississippi, the Whole of the Illinois River, Lake Erie, Part of the Lakes Huron, Michigan, &c., and all the Country bordering on these Lakes and Rivers".* (From a 1904 special edition of the English language edition of the author's *Topographical Description.* Cleveland: Burrow Bros.). **[16b]**

Hutchins accompanied expeditions to the Mississippi at the time of Pittman's own travels into the Illinois Country as a young officer and produced his own accounts of these journeys with excellent maps which are among the earliest—if not the earliest—printed maps with St. Louis clearly identified in a location long known to some explorers, obscured or overlooked by others for one hundred years of mapping New France. Many of these descriptive narratives borrow heavily from Pittman, but his maps are crucial for the period he describes. Much later, Hutchins was an important surveyor for the territories of the young United States, rising to the post of Geographer to the United States, the first and only citizen ever to hold such a position.

[16a]

PLAN des Villages de la Contrée DES ILLINOIS et partie de la Riviere de Mißißipi par Hutchins.

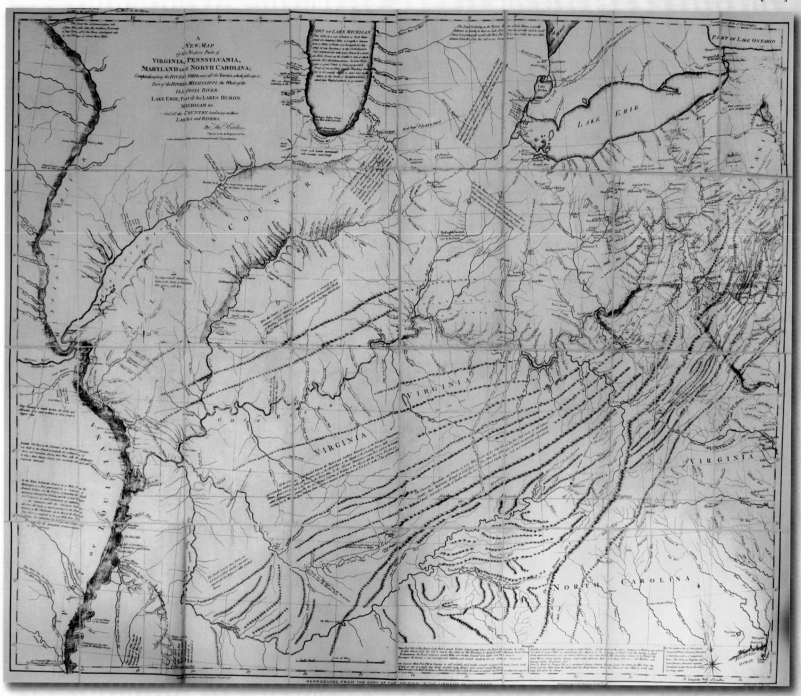

33

17 Gilbert Imlay. *A Map of the Western Part of Territories belonging to the United States of America, Drawn from the best Authorities.*
London: Debrett, 1795. (From Imlay's *A Topographical Description of the Western Territory of North America*. London: Debrett, 1797). **[17]** With **[Fig. a]**: Abel Buell's *New and Correct Map of the United States of North America*. New Haven, 1784 (New Jersey State Historical Society, undated facsimile [ca. 1961]).

These are two of the earliest American maps with St. Louis printed on them after Hutchins. Imlay and Buell are both colorful figures who influenced the growth of the United States profoundly with such promotional pieces, far in excess of what may have been felt their potential by their own contemporaries. The young United States was populated with memorable entrepreneurial characters, and those involved with emigration schemes and land deals rubbed shoulders with ease with serious engineers and geographers to get the word out (for personal gain as much a anything else) about the vast opening of a continent, to a determined and invested American reading public.

[Fig. a]

A NEW AND CORRECT MAP OF THE UNITED STATES OF

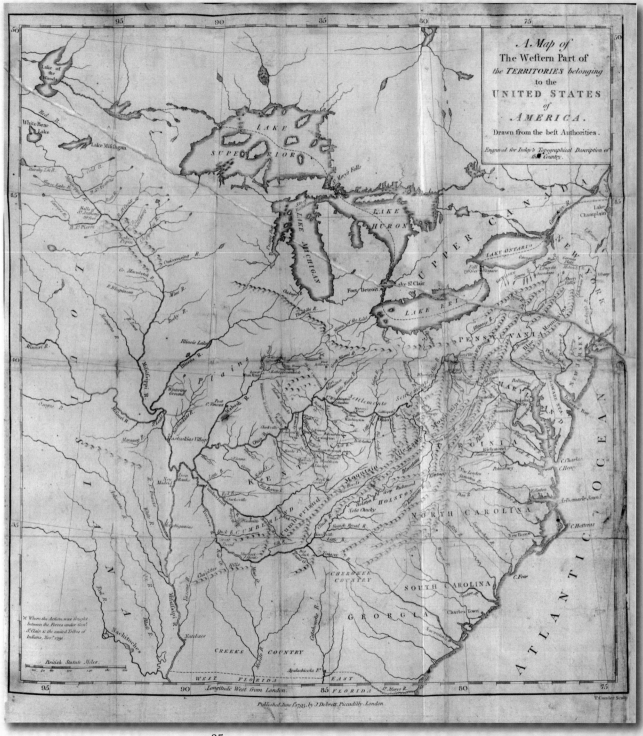

17

18

Guy Dufossat. *Map of the Mississippi River from Pain-Court (St. Louis) to Cold Water Rock.* Copy of a manuscript map from 1767 prepared by Norbury Wayman, Wayman Collection, St. Louis Mercantile Library. The earliest known map which shows the Village of St. Louis. **[18a]** With a manuscript copy by Wayman of a copy of the 1780 plan of St. Louis redrawn in later times by Auguste Chouteau: *Saint Louis des Ilinois.* **[18b]**

The original maps of St. Louis were lost to time—a few manuscript tracings related to official works and expeditions exist in colonial archives in Madrid or Paris, with a few other plans surviving in a handful of historical societies and libraries such as the Mercantile Library and the Missouri History Museum as well as specific maps existing from the earliest days of the 19th century existing in St. Louis City and County collections. The Mercantile Library, along with preserving a few of these precious original manuscripts also has a large collection of tracings of plans and plats which were created in the early 20th century, forming a useful study collection. These two early maps show the beginning of a typical French colonial town situated on excellent, elevated ground, protected from floods. The village was a fur trading post first and foremost at the beginning, but the town was so well afforded fields, fresh water and an abundance of resources to be capable of building a strong, sustainable village regardless, so that its early nickname of "Pain-Court" to travelers (due to settlers' reticence at first to operate plows and gristmills) did not stick.

[18a]

[18b]

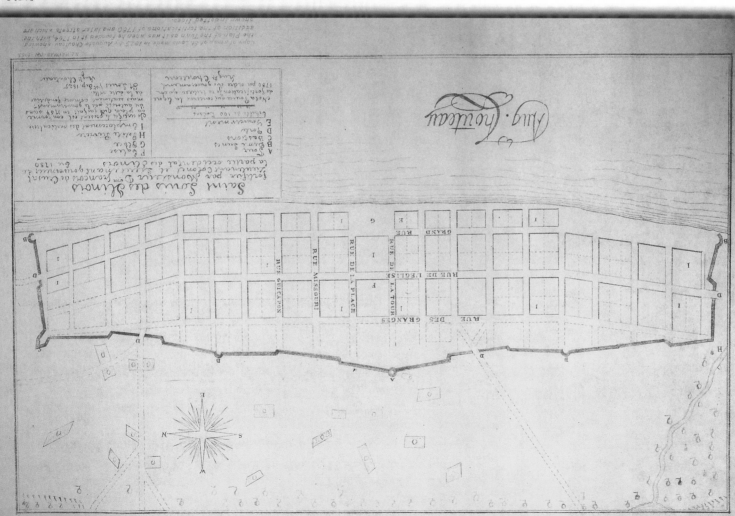

Indian of the Nation of the Shawanoes.

[Fig. c]

Indian of the Nation of the Kaskaskia.

[Fig. b]

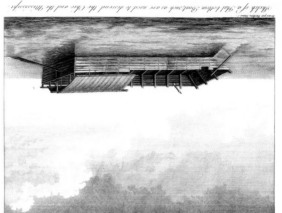

[Fig. d]

Model of a flat Indian Boat, such as are used to descend the Ohio and the Mississippi.

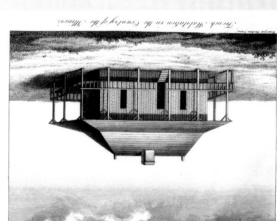

French Habitation in the Country of the Illinois.

[Fig. a]

19

George H. V. Victor Collot. ***Plan of St. Lewis, With the Project of an Intrenched Camp French.*** Voyage dans l'Amérique Septentrionale ou Description des Pays arroses par le Mississipi, l'Ohio, le Missouri, et autres Rivieres Affluentes &c. Paris: Bertrand, 1826. **[19a]** With *Map of the Country of the Illinois.* **[19b]**

Collot's maps of Louisiana were made in 1796 and were most likely planned for military intrigues and colonial conquest, but the work transcended its purpose in thoroughly documenting the earliest settlements of the Illinois Country. These plans were the most detailed to their time. **[Fig. a]**: *"French Habitation in the Country of the Illinois"*; **[Fig. b]**: *"Indian of the Nation of the Kaskaskia"*; **[Fig. c]**: *"Indian of the Nation of the Shawanoes"*; **[Fig. d]**: *"Sketch of a Flat bottom Boat, such as are used to descend the Ohio and the Mississipi".*

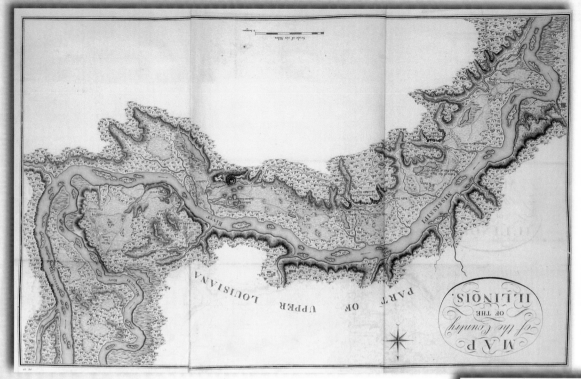

[19b]

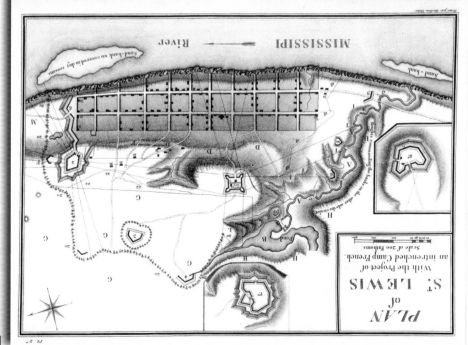

[19a]

20

Francois Marie Perrin Du Lac. *Carte du Missouri Levee ou Rectisiee dans toute son Etendue.* From *Voyage dans les deux Louisiannes et chez les nations sauvages du Missouri &c.* Paris Capelle et Renard, 1805. **[20a]**

A map drawn in 1802 based on information gained in St. Louis about the vast lands outward from the city in all directions. With four great American maps showing the city by the turn of the 19th century at the headwaters of greatness and grand ambition: Patrick Gass' *"Carte Pour server au Voyage des Capes. Lewis et Clark a l'Ocean Pacifique".* From Gass' 1810 account of the expedition, supplying the first map of the monumental journey; **[20b]** also with *"A Map of Lewis and Clark's Track across the Western Portions of North America, from the Mississippi to the Pacific Ocean"* which appeared in 1814 in *Travels to the Source of the Missouri River;* **[20c]** also with Zebulon Pike's *"Map of the Mississippi River from its Source to the Mouth of the Missouri"* **[20d]** and the unusual perspective of Pike's *"The*

First Part of Capt. Pike's Chart of the Internal Part of Louisiana" **[20e]**, both from Pike's *An Account of Expeditions to the Sources of the Mississippi, and through the Western Parts of Louisiana to the Sources of the Arkansaw, Kans, La Platte and Pierre Juan Rivers.* (Philadelphia: Conrad, 1810). All of these maps start with St. Louis, and fulfill the dreams of another nation's wish for empire but now for a younger nation of new cities and lands, based but steeped in an earlier time. A final example of this placement of the city as a capital of a western province would be Prince Maximilian of Wied-Neuwied's 1830s map here showing the detail of St. Louis in relation to its proud territorial stakes and ambitions. **[Fig. a]**

[Fig. a]

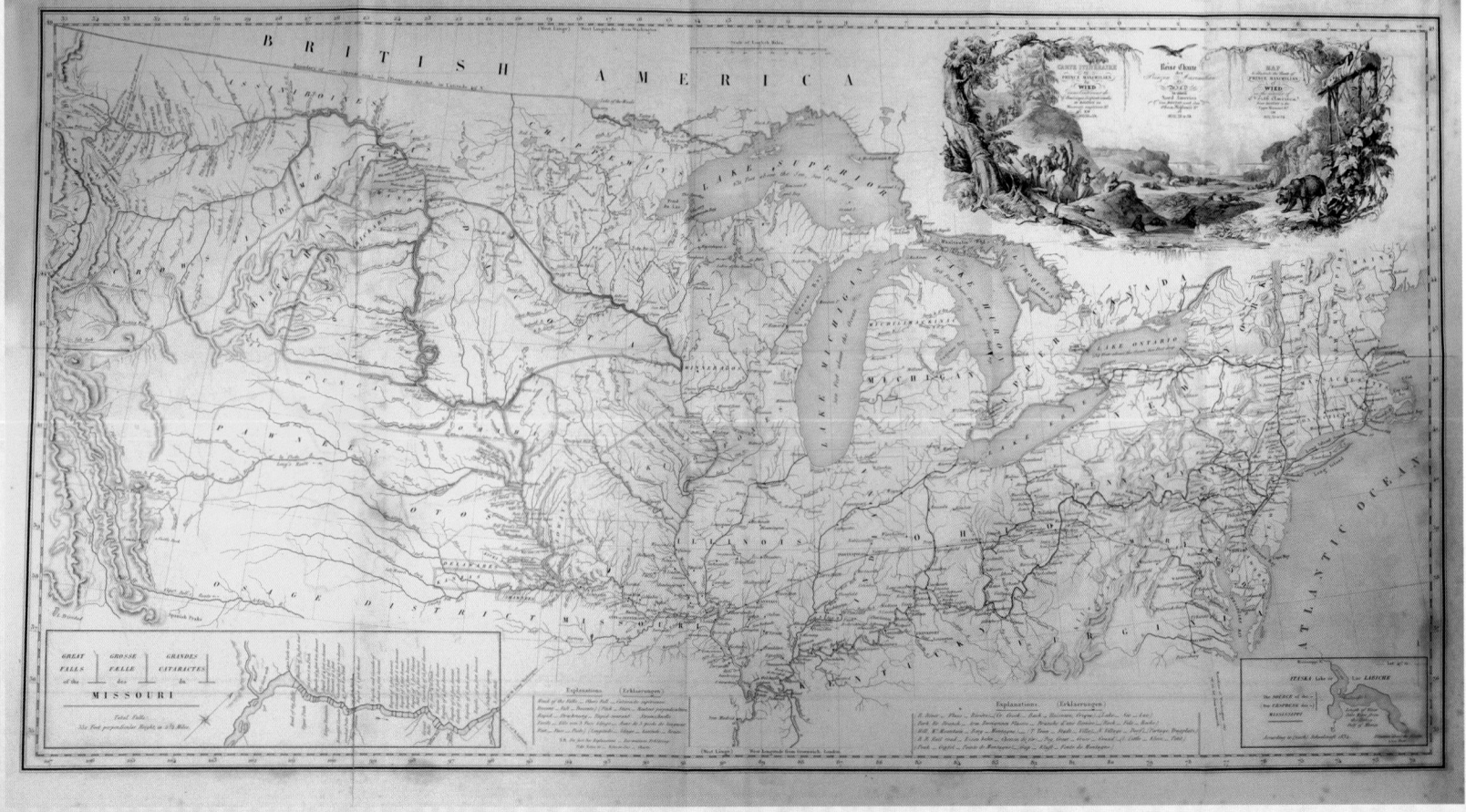

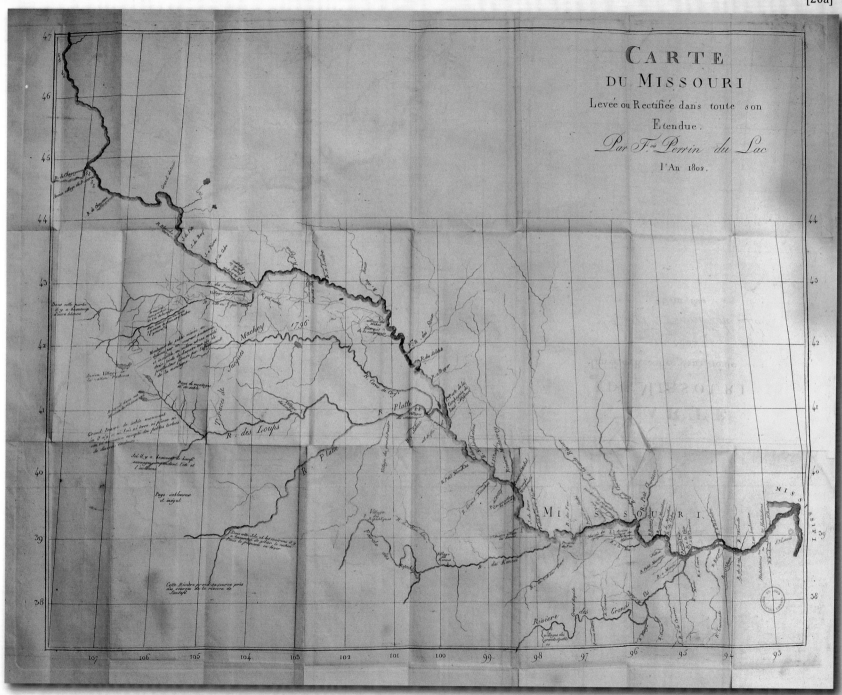

CARTE
DU MISSOURI
Levée ou Rectifiée dans toute son
Etendue.
Par F.ois Perrin du Lac.
l'An 1802.

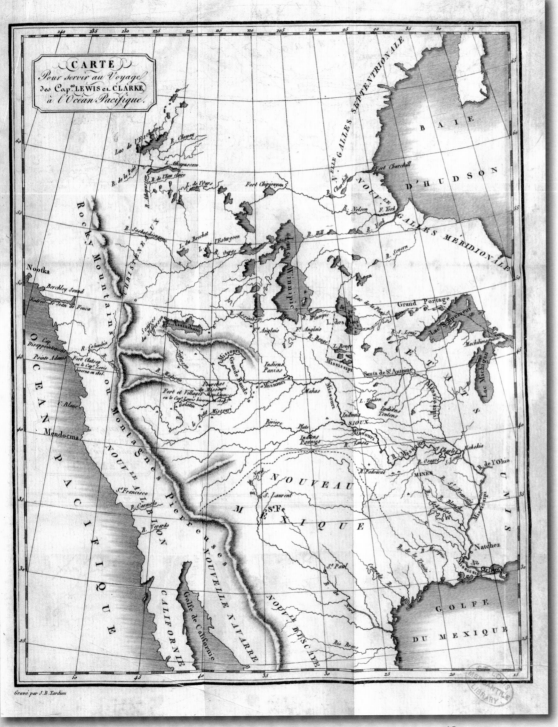

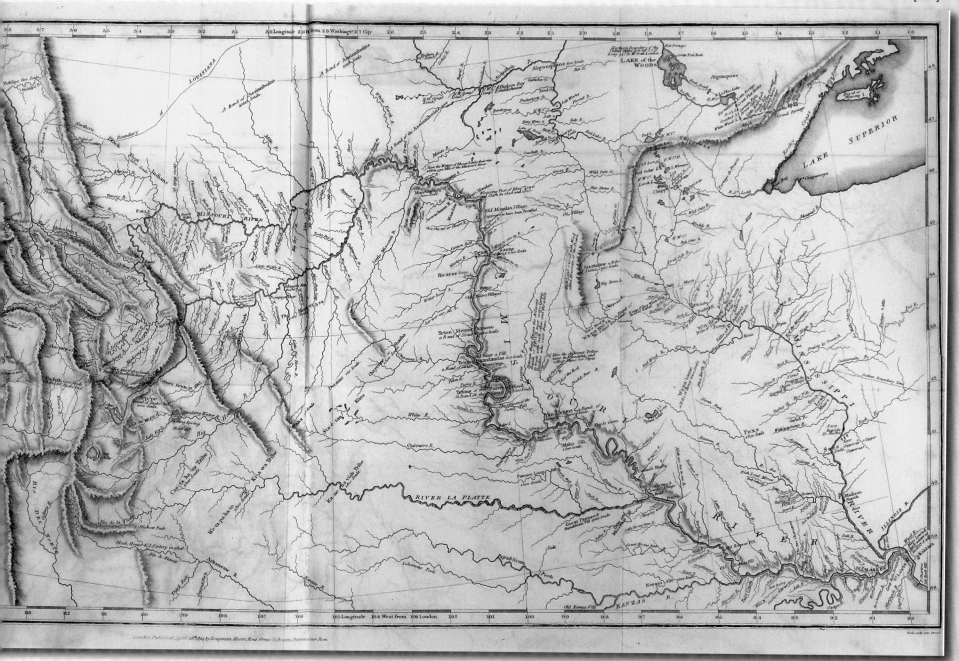

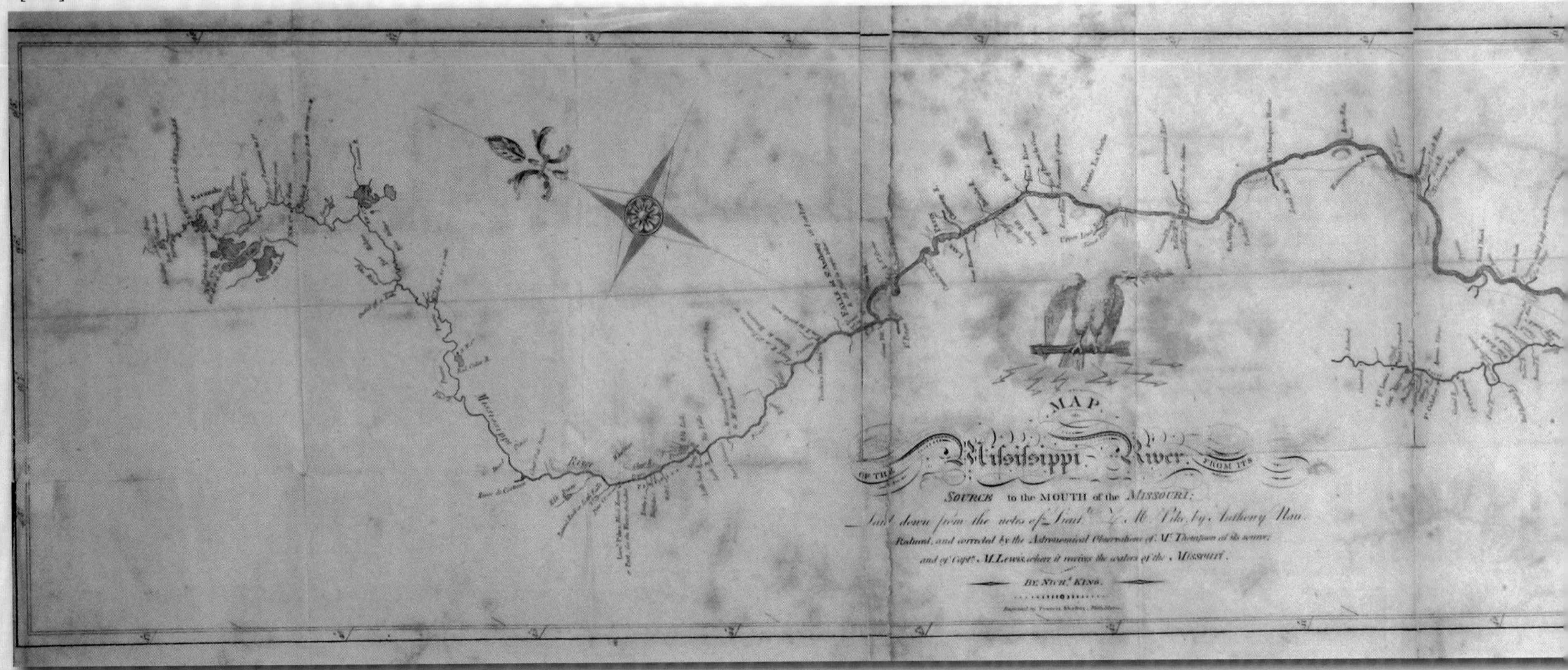

MAP
OF THE
Mississippi River, FROM ITS
SOURCE to the MOUTH of the MISSOURI;
laid down from the notes of Lieut. Z. M. Pike, by Anthony Nau.
Reduced, and corrected by the Astronomical Observations of Mr. Thompson at its source;
and of Capt. M. Lewis, where it receives the waters of the Missouri.
BY NICH. KING.

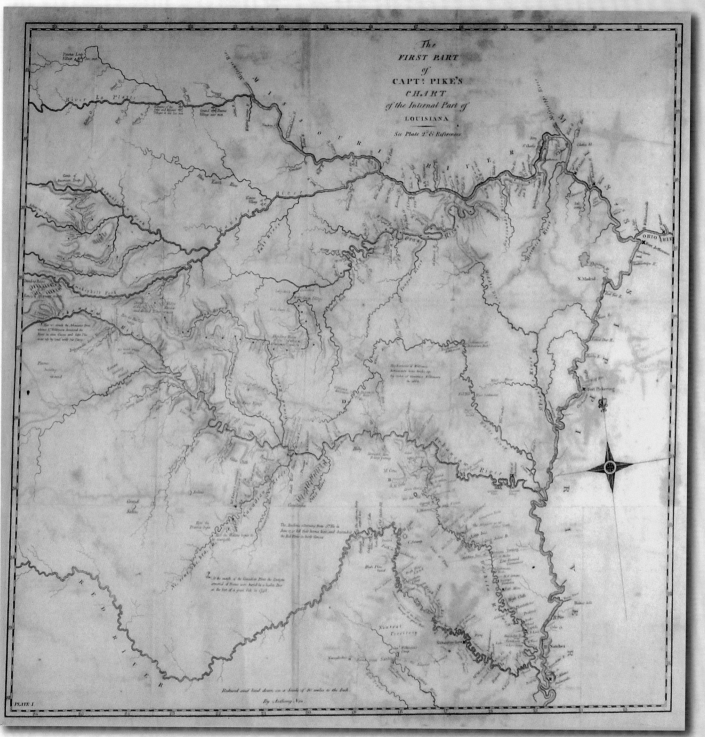

[20e]

Part Two:

A City and its State: Mapping Missouri from Territorial Days to the Twentieth Century.
The Map of Missouri Anchored by St. Louis.

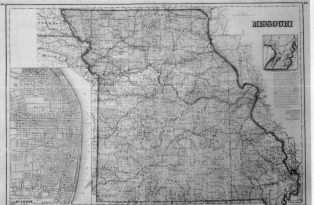

[Fig. a]

Long before Missouri appeared as a territory or state on the national map of the young United States, it existed, through its namesake river, as the land and water highway of St. Louis. The city and state developed together, geographically, politically, economically and administratively. It was almost as if a state needed to be invented for St. Louis to move its traders, flatboats and wagons, later trains, steamboats and airplanes from end to end and outward. The old Missouri maps often showed a prominent inset of the growing city of St. Louis, a regular design repeatedly used for centuries in this marriage of state and city. **[Fig. a]**; also with *"Entrance of the Traders into Santa Fe"* from *Commerce of the Prairie* **[Fig. b]**; and *Jolly Flat Boat Men* after Bingham **[Fig. c]**.

[Fig. b]

21   Jacques Bellin. ***Carte de la Louisiane et Pays Voisins.*** From Prevost d'Exiles' *Histoire Generale des Voiages*. Paris: Didot, 1757 **[21a]**; with Thomas Pownall's *"A Map of the Middle British Colonies in North America by Mr. Lewis Evans of Philadelphia in 1755; and since Corrected and Improved as also Extended with the Addition of New England and Bordering Parts of Canada; from Actual Surveys now Lying at the Board of Trade"*. From *A Topographical Description of Such Parts of North America as are Contained in the (Annexed) Map of the Middle British Colonies, &c. in North America*. London: J. Almon, 1776 **[21b]**; and Pownall's *"A New Map of North America with the West India Islands Divided According to the Preliminary Articles of Peace, Signed at Versailles, 20 Jan., 1783 wherein are Particularly Distinguished the United States etc."* London: Laurie & Whittle, 1794 **[21c]**.

[Fig. c]

These maps are some of the most accurate claims and counterclaims from the time of the French and Indian War to the end of the American Revolution, with what would become Missouri at the center of these rivalries. Bellin restated cartographically French borders before vast territories were ceded away and lost—Pownall and the British surveyors of the late 18th century were presenting a new world in his maps of English speaking settlement across immense territories. Note the inset in the 1776 map, almost greedily depicting the Upper Mississippi Valley's west bank to the St. Louis region.

[21a]

[21b]

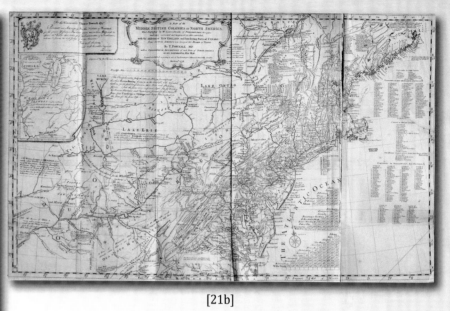

[21c]

22 Antonio Zatta. *Il Paese de' Cherachesi, con la Parte Occidentale della Carolina Setenttrionale, e della Virginia.* 1778. From *Le Colonie Unite dell' America Settentrionale*. Venice: Zatta, 1778. **[22]**

This map and the atlas in which it appeared were based on the important map by John Mitchell, one of the earliest English mapmakers to give an accurate representation of the Missouri and the central river system of the mid continent. Mitchell's maps were influential for a century and, as seen here, were appreciated by an international following of mapmakers.

IL PAESE DE' CHERACHESI, CON LA PARTE OCCIDENTALE DELLA CAROLINA SETTENTRIONALE, E DELLA VIRGINIA.

Fte. Orleans

Missouri F.

Missouris

Stagno salato

Misouri F.

Osages F.

Osages

Piccoli Osages

Ragnac F.

Fiume Conza

Kansez Fiume

Ranju Fiume

Rupe

Paese pieno di Miniere

Maramec Fiume

Miniere di Maramec che diedero occasione al famoso piano del Misisipi nel 1719

Pagunine F.

Piaho Fiume

Bles Fiume

Vermillion Fiume

Fiume S. Francesco

Confin del Ouest

1170 miglia lungi dalla foce del Misisipi per acqua

Fiume Emisour

MISSISIPI F.

Kahokes

la Tamaroas Fte. e Missione

Metchiagamie

Fte. Chartres

Miniere della Motte

Saline

Saline Fiume

Kaskakies 140 miglia

Isla Grande

C. S. Antonio

Forchi del Misisipi

V. la Nazione de Illinois...

Il FIUME OHIO largo circa un miglio con 5, o 6 belle aqua verso le cascate

VIRGINIA

Wawaughtanese Fiume

Pyankachees

Piccolo Wiautes

Wabache Fiume

I primi Stabilimenti degl'Inglesi dell'Ohie erano sopra l'Alligany, ma da 50 anni in qua si sono estesi da Chenango a Pickawillany

Estensione de Stabilimenti Inglesi

3 Forche

Fiume Mad

Strada principale de Maurists

Fiume dell'Ouest

la Damoiselle

Piccolo Maramec Fiume

Rivers Pond ov. Stagno Castor Mianis

Cuttawa

Cumberland Fiume

Gran Pianura fertilissima secondo le relazioni degl' Indiani ed Inglesi

Walkers

Estensione de Stabilimenti Inglesi nel 1750

Fiume Chinds

Holston

Fiume Rito Storto

Isole della Stretto

Fatti 920 m. lungi dal Mare

Fiume dei Cherakeii ov. Hogohege F.

LUIGIANA

MISSISIPE F.

CAROLINA SETT.

CHERAKESI

Il Paese dei Cherakesi che si stende sino al Misisipi verso l'Ouest, terminato al Nord verso li confini del le 5 Nazioni, fu rimesso all'Inghilterra formalmente a Westminster l'anno 1729.

F. Hogokegee ov. Callamaco

Telliquo

Questo Fiume è navigabile sino a questa cascata

Cherakesi Superiori

Cherakee

Chotte

Telliquo F.

SPAGNUOLA

Mentos

Fiume Bianco

Isole Candelaria

Kappa era un Forte Francese il loro più alto stabilimento

CHICACHESI
Alleati e soggetti agl'Inglesi

Cherakesi di MEZZO

Euphasee

Ameyie

Quanesee
Fattoria Inglese

Cherakesi

Naquasee

Fiume degli Akansas

23 Joseph Scott. *A Map of the United States.* From Scott's *The United States Gazetteer Containing an Authentic Description of the Several States.* Philadelphia: Bailey, 1795 **[23a]**; with a map of the United States in *Neele's General Atlas, Consisting of a Complete Set of Maps from the Best Authorities and Including all New Discoveries.* London: Samuel and George Neele and Longman, Hurst, Rees, Orme, & Brown, 1814 **[23b]**.

Two maps which burden Louisiana and the soon to be Missouri Territory with misinformation and lack of recognition of American claims. Very little is shown to be known west of the Mississippi in Scott's popular Gazetteer. Jefferson needed better sources for an eventual land deal than this, such as Jonathan Carver, French maps, Hutchins, Pownall and others. When one looks at the popular British Neele atlas published at the time of the collapse of Napoleonic Europe, it is clear that the President and his successors needed Clark's and Pike's maps in print as quickly as possible to reinforce valid ownership of an immense piece of ground.

[23a]

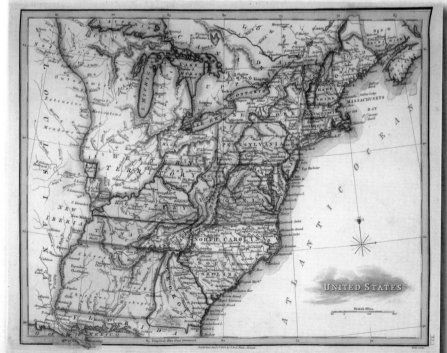

[23b]

51

24 John Melish. *Map of the United States with the Contiguous British and Spanish Possessions.* Philadelphia: Melish, 1818 (1816). [24]

Melish's great map served the young American nation well—and Missouri and St. Louis also as seats of power and administration. Here most of the Louisiana Purchase, in fact, has been designated "Missouri Territory" and the proto boundaries of the state begin to appear in a faint outline—a high northern boundary into later Iowa, a large tract of Arkansas territory and the beginnings of the familiar "boot heel" of Missouri, outlined by Ozark mountain ranges and river bluffs (the concept originally extending southward), if not actual legal boundary lines. This is a map of extraordinary beauty, usefulness and historical significance, extending at a very early time the concept of an American nation to the Pacific. The map found its way in all the schools and libraries of the early Republic, and has been influential to the present day.

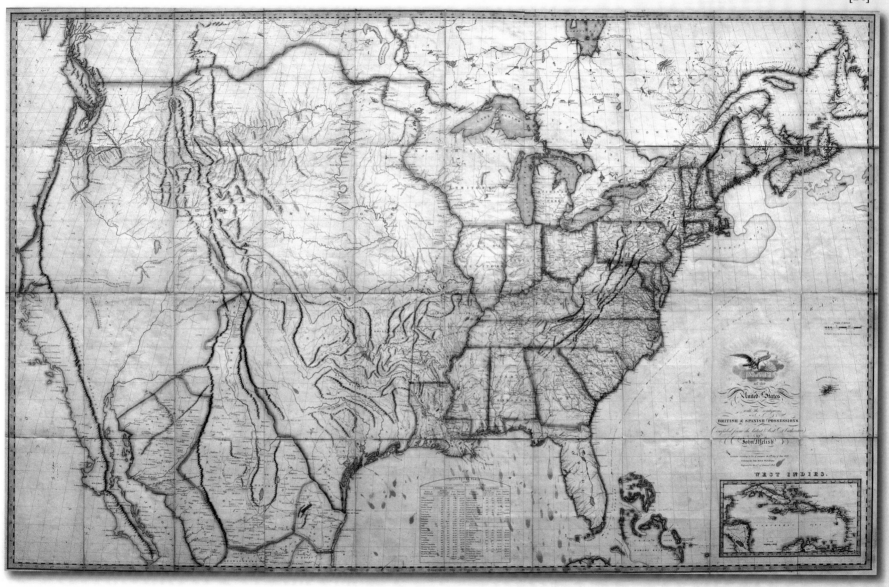

24

25

Pablo Alabern i Moles. *Estados Unidos de la America Septentrional.* Barcelona, 1820. [25]

An early European map showing the origin of all the major rivers in one high elevation, still strongly viewed as a possibility in the unexplored territories. The young United States, including Missouri and Arkansas, are outlined in yellow—"Missiri" is the territorial name, "Sn. Luis" is the name used for the state of Missouri. The Pacific Northwest is outlined in blue as "Colombia" and, again, most of the Louisiana Territory, as "Missiri", in red.

ESTADOS UNIDOS
de la América Septentrional.

Longitud oriental de Madrid.

26

John Gardiner. ***Map of the Bounty Lands of the Illinois Territory.*** Washington, 1818 **[26a]**; with Gardiner's similar and equally important *"Map of the Northern Part of Missouri Territory"*, 1818 **[26b]**.

These maps were produced by Gardiner as Chief Clerk of the General Land Office of the United States under pressure by Congress to begin the sale of "bounty lands" cheaply to veterans of past wars in recognition of military service rendered. The Missouri map is the first official United States survey of any territory in the trans-Mississippi west. The Illinois map, which is of western Illinois to the Missouri River confluence, is a remarkable survival, signed by Gardiner in distributing, verifying and describing a new settler's plot: "Description of the SE of section 35 in township 4N of range 7 West. A stream in the quarter section, part gently rolling woodland and good soil, part level, Rich prairie; Timber Oak & Hickory underwood, Hazel. Your lot is black in the yellow township."

[26a]

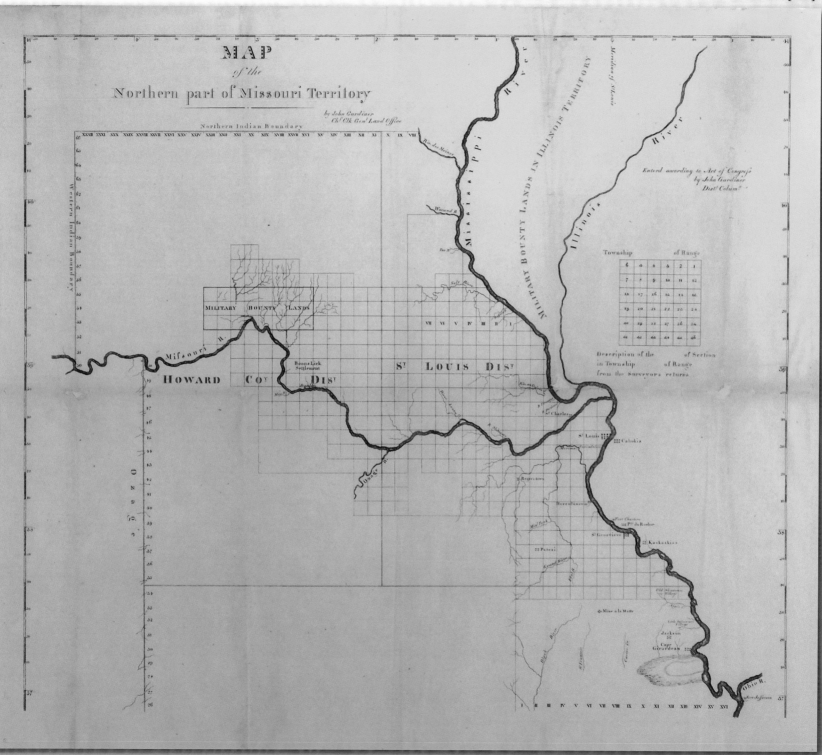

MAP

of the

Northern part of Missouri Territory

by John Gardiner
Ch.f Clk Gen.l Land Office

27 **Map of Missouri.** From *The Historical, Chronological and Geographical American Atlas.* Philadelphia: Carey and Lea: 1823 **[27a]**; with the Buchon, Carez, and Beaupre *Carte geographique, statistique et historique du Missouri.* Paris: Carez, 1825 from those authors' general atlas in French and essentially the same map **[27b]**; with *"Map of the State of Missouri and Territory of Arkansas"* from the pocket edition of Anthony Finley's *A New American Atlas* published in Philadelphia in 1826 as engraved by Young and Delleker in 1826 **[27c]** shown with the splendidly detailed tracings **[Fig. a]** of *"Map of North America"* from the same atlas.

These maps show Missouri at the time of statehood in 1820, the age in fact of the seeds of the Civil War in the Missouri Compromise. Here Missouri is shown as the largest state in the Union; the Finley North American map shows the Missouri Territory to its fullest imagined extent. All of these maps present the growing detail and interest of map makers for this potential bread basket, crossroads and highly politicized region.

[Fig. a]

58

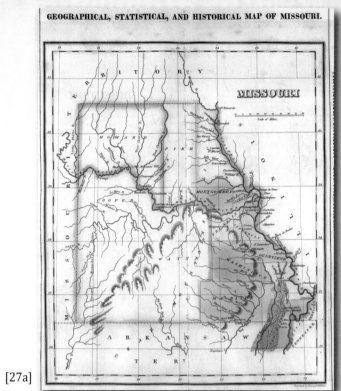

GEOGRAPHICAL, STATISTICAL, AND HISTORICAL MAP OF MISSOURI.

[27a]

[27b]

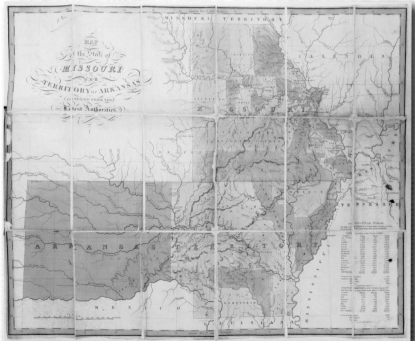

[27c]

59

28 H. Selves. *Carte des Etats-Unis, a l'usage des Colleges.* From *Atlas Geographique dresse sous la Direction du Conseil Royal de l'instruction publique pour l'usage des colleges. Paris: Selves, 1832* **[28a]**; with Charles Varle's wall map of the United States, published by the Stebbins Co. in 1834 **[28b]**.

The first of these maps was from a French school atlas which gave clear information on names of waterways, lakes, mountain ranges, native tribes, along with cities and states. The trans-Mississippi, in an interesting French administrative style, is drawn up in districts, the earliest western state, of Missouri, being in the "Ozark district". If there were ever two maps as this one from Paris, and Varles', a reference map probably intended for colleges as well as one-room schoolhouses, that showed better the state of Missouri as the mother of the American West, they would have stiff competition from such maps like these.

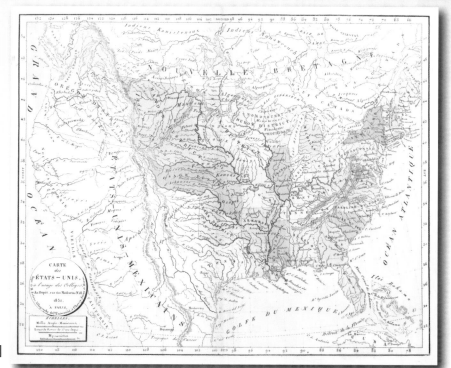

[28a]

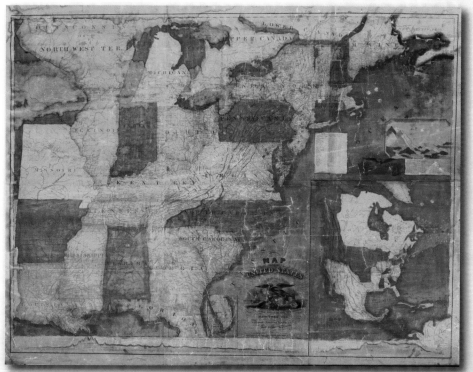

[28b]

29 George A. Leakin. *Map Showing the Disputed Boundary of Missouri and Iowa. 27th US Congress, 3rd Session, House of Rep. Doc. #38.* Washington: Stone, 1842 **[29a]** with other Boundary maps and diagrams of the 1830s and 1840s including *Diagram of the State of Missouri.* St. Louis: Surveyor's Office, 1837 **[29b]**; Meriwether Lewis Clark's *Diagram of the State of Missouri.* St. Louis, 1849 **[29c]** and Conway's *Diagram of the State of Missouri.* 1849 **[29d]** with Alphonso Wetmore's map in his *Gazetteer of the State of Missouri.* St. Louis: Keemle, 1837 **[29e]** and **[Fig. a]**: the wild frontispiece from this gazetteer of a bear hunt and **[Fig. b]**: David Burr's *"Map of Missouri: from the New and Universal Atlas Comprising Separate Maps of all the Empires, Kingdoms and States throughout the World and Forming a Distinct Atlas of the United States".* New York: Stone, 1836.

These maps depict the steps officials in Missouri and Iowa took to create two modern states. They were landmarks in their day—actually led to possible armed conflict in the "Honey War" on the contested state line or lines, when several honey bee tree hives were cut done—militias and hot heads assembled on both sides of the supposed boundaries. Iowa got a proper line and eventually Missouri got the Platte district and stretched toward Council Bluffs and the Missouri River country's rich soil in the northwest. Much of the work for the resolution of this conflict was performed out of St. Louis in the 1830s, but these maps show the evolution of the state's familiar boundary lines evocatively.

[Fig. a]

[Fig. b]

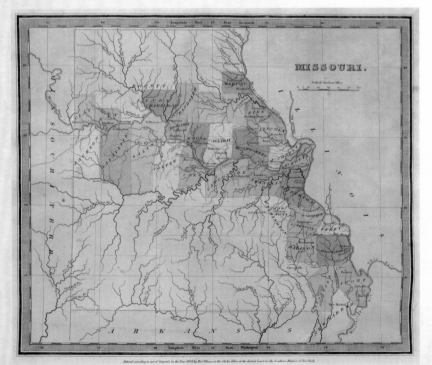

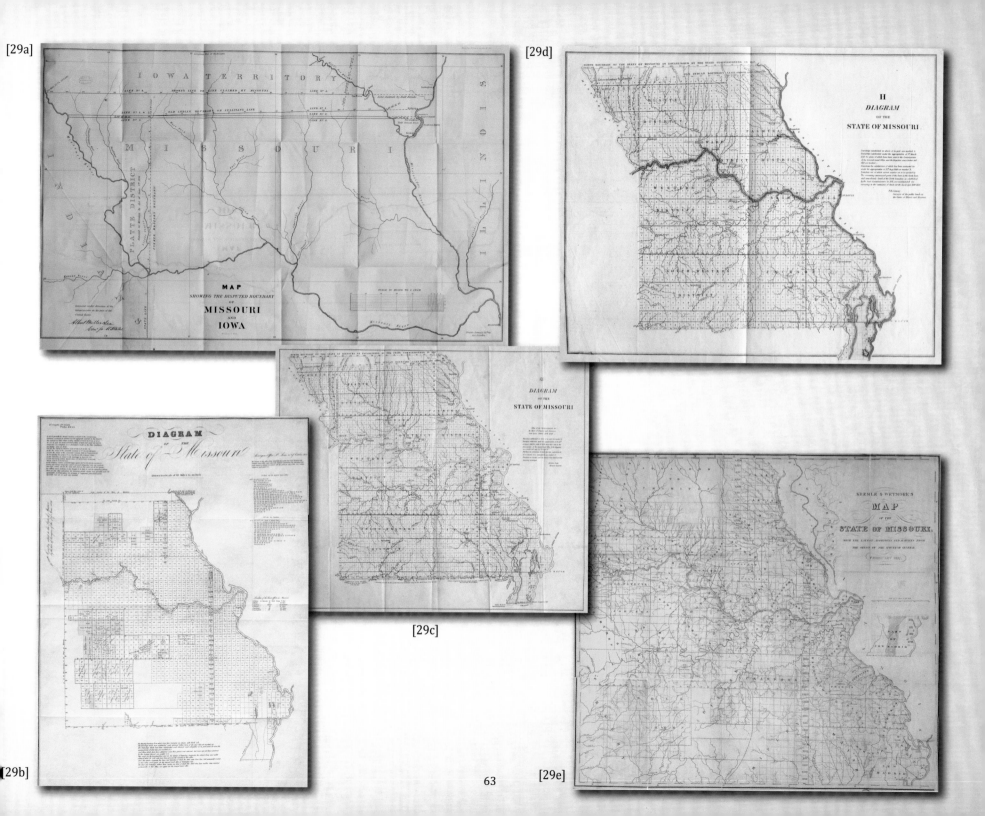

[29a]

[29d]

[29c]

[29b]

[29e]

30

School geographies of the mid 19th century. The map of the United States in T. G. Bradford's *A Comprehensive Atlas Geographical (Boston: Wilkins and Carter, 1843)* **[30a]** is accurate for the most part about the region but the boundaries are still shown in dispute in the map of *Missouri, Illinois and Iowa.* **[Fig. a]**; *Illinois and Missouri* is interesting placed next to a map and descriptive section on *Texas*, in many ways a state in St. Louis' age-old economic trading sphere, from Sidney Morse's *System of Geography for the Use of Schools (New York: Harper and Brothers, 1845)* **[30b]** with the *Map of the Western States and Territories from Mitchell's Primary Geography)Philadelphia: Cowperthwaite, 1852)*, a textbook intended for instruction of children by Augustus Mitchell **[30c]**.

On the eve of the Civil War the early national school geographies seemed to reinforce sectionalism in these clear and plainly read maps.

[Fig. a]

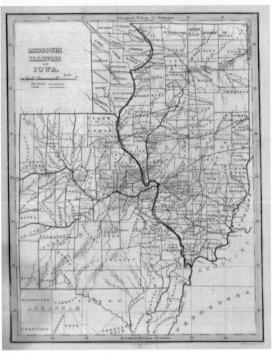

[30a]

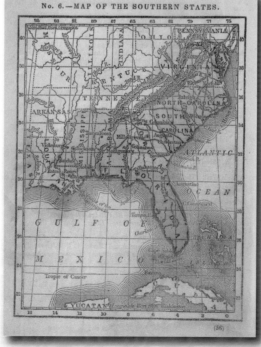

31 *Lloyd's 1863 Map of the Southern States Showing all the Railroads, their Stations and Distances; also the Counties, Towns, Villages, their Stations and Distances, Compiled from the Latest Government and Other Reliable Sources.* New York: J. T. Lloyd, Publisher, 1863 **[31a]**; with A. J. Johnson, *"Missouri and Kansas"*, 1864 **[31b]**; also with *"Fiala and Heren's New Sectional Map of the State of Missouri"* St. Louis: Gray and Crawford, 1861 **[31c]** with small contemporary map of battles in Missouri during the Civil War **[Fig. a]** and E. Leigh's *"A View of the Slave Population of the Several Counties of Missouri, Showing the Whole Number of Slaves in Each County"* from *Bird's Eye Views of Slavery in Missouri*. St. Louis: Woods et al, 1862. **[Fig. b]**. A. J. Johnsons map also showed the east/west population movement along trails and rails to heavily developed eastern Kansas, from his 1864 *New Illustrated Family Atlas.* **[31d].**

Missouri was an important battleground during the Civil War and these maps show many reasons why it was crucial to remain part of the Union at all cost. The magnificent railroad map published by J. T. Lloyd was a strategic war map, a way the public could anticipate defenses and military operations surrounding the lifelines of the populations served by the rails. This is an excellent map, in detail of the railroad in St. Louis before the coming of the Eads Bridge across the Mississippi, the first great rail bridge linking east and west in the 1870s. The sectional map of Missouri shows as well at the time of conflict the growing map printing industry in St. Louis itself. The remarkable maps by Leigh show visually that Missouri was not split over slavery north to south or east to west, from 1820 and before, slavery followed the Missouri River valley and rich agricultural and industrial heartland of the state out of St. Louis, straight to Kansas City.

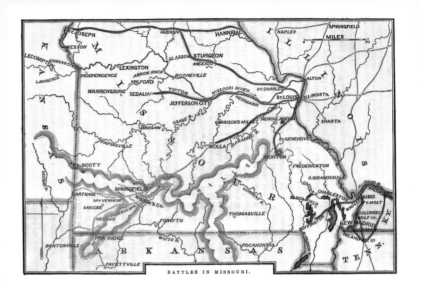

[Fig. a]

[Fig. b]

[31a]

[31b]

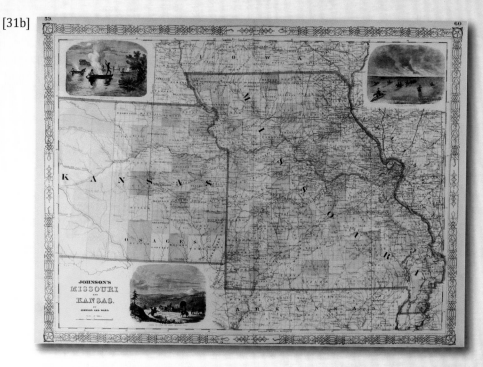

[31c]

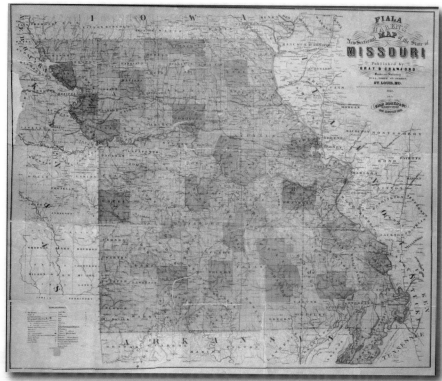

[31d]

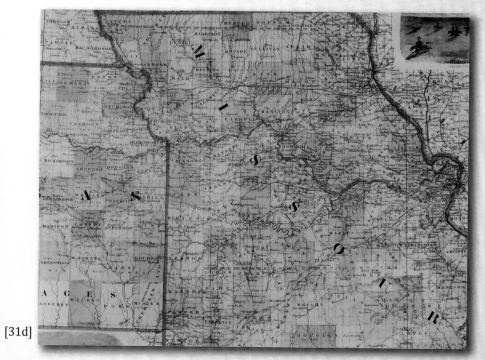

32

Missouri and Arkansas from *Black's General Atlas of the World*. Edinburgh: Adam and Charles Black, 1867 **[32a]** with the official map of the *State of Missouri* in 1866, from the *Maps Accompanying Report of the Commissioner of the General Land Office* **[32b]** with *"Political Map of Missouri"* from *Campbell's New Atlas of Missouri*. St. Louis: R. A. Campbell, 1873 **[32c]**.

After the war and before the industrialization of Missouri, these maps depict a state and its cities and counties in full growth and developmental potential. The Blacks were a pair of publishers of annual atlases and well designed world travel books. The commissioner's report can be looked at instructively for the fast development of the state, from Gardiner's early surveys (item **[26]**). This was the beginning of the age of county, and even more elaborate, illustrated state atlases across the United States, and Campbell's *Atlas* was no exception to the promotion that such works provided for future economic development.

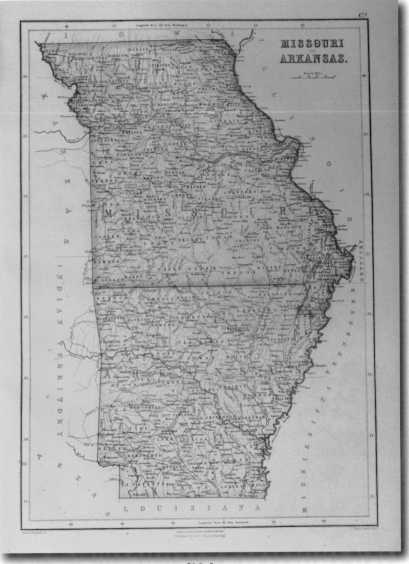

[32a]

[32b]

[32c]

33

G. C. Broadhead. *Preliminary Geological Map of Northern Missouri*, 1873 **[33a]**; with *"Geodetic Connection of the Atlantic and Pacific Coast Triangulations, Illinois and Missouri"*. 1877 **[33b]**; and also with the maps of *Mineral Resources of Missouri*. Missouri Geological Survey, 1944 and 1988 **[33c, 33d]**.

Broadhead's map was one of the first to recognize the stark divisions of Missouri's geography. Located so close to the center of the continent, it was a point of great scientific interest to geologists and even the geodetic surveys of the 19th century. These distinct areas came to be known as the Northern Plains, the Ozark Plateau and the Mississippi Alluvial Plain and were well represented on such beautiful scientific maps for the state through the generations.

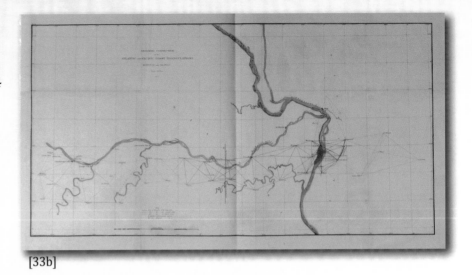

[33b]

[33a]

[33c]

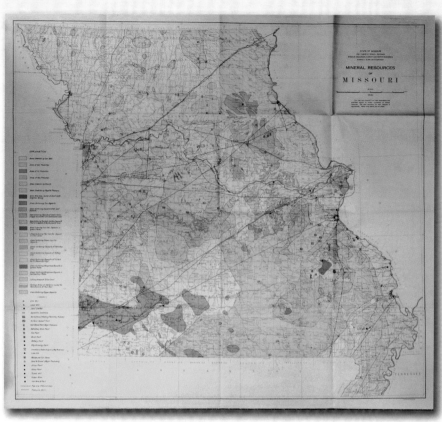

[33d]

71

34

Missouri. Chicago: Rand McNally, 1880 **[34a]** with the Rand McNally and Co.'s *"New Sectional Map of Missouri"*. 1884 **[34b]** and with Willard C. Hall. Labor Commissioners *"Official Map of Missouri"*. 1891 **[34c]** and with the well used roll map *"Higgins Sectional and Roadmap of Missouri"*. St. Louis: Higgins and Co., 1898 **[see Fig. detail]**.

Maps of Missouri at the turn of the twentieth century developed on further thematic lines and related emphatically labor and urbanization with the metropolis of St. Louis prominently marked. The Higgins Co. was another of the St. Louis map producers, prominent throughout the coming decades.

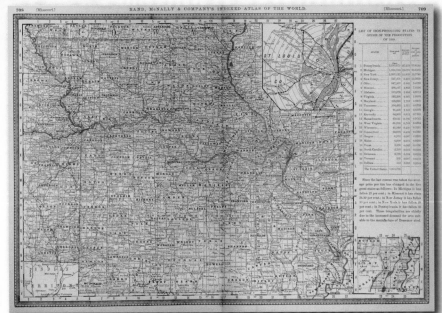

[34a]

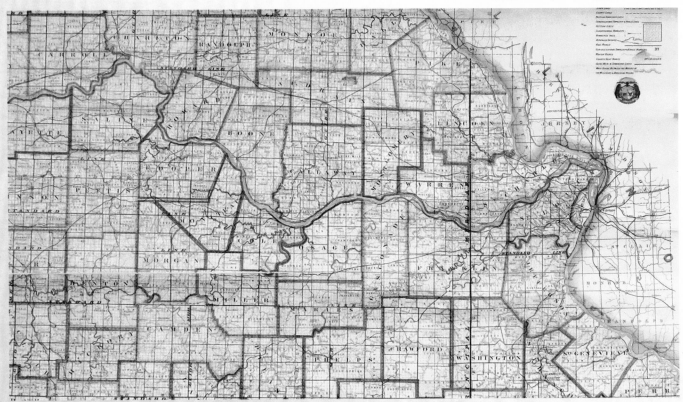

[Fig. detail]

[34b]

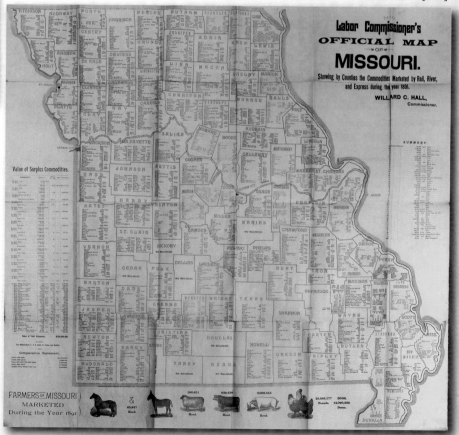

[34c]

73

35

Map of the Pacific Rail Road of Missouri and its Connections.
From J. West Goodwin. *Pacific Railway Business Guide & Gazetteer of Missouri and Kansas.* St. Louis, 1867 **[35a]** with John Breathitt's *"Commissioners Official Railway Map of Missouri"*, 1891 **[35b]** with the same map republished in St. Louis by Higgins & Co. in 1902 **[35c]**; with other railroad maps related to Missouri and St. Louis history: J. L. Tracy's *"The Latest, Best, and Cheapest Township Map of Missouri with Tables of Stations, Distances, and Connections for all Railroads Leading out of St. Louis"*. St. Louis: R. P. Studley & Co., 1871 **[35d]**; the Rand McNally *"Commercial Atlas Standard Map of Missouri"*, 1935 **[Fig. a]**; *"Map of the Missouri Pacific Lines"*, 1929 **[Fig. b]**; the Reconstruction and Finance Commission *"Map of Corporate Ownership for the St. Louis-San Francisco Railway"*; 1939 **[Fig. c]**; *"Map of the Southern Pacific Lines"*, undated, mid-20th century **[Fig. d]**; *"Burlington Northern Missouri State Railroad Map"*, 1983 **[35e]**; the Woodward and Tiernan time table *"Map of the Missouri Pacific Through Line and Connections"*; St. Louis, late 19th Century **[Fig. e]**.

The storied history of rail development out of St. Louis and across the west and southwest is stirring, full of triumph and exuberant language and pride—the first state with the backing of St. Louis financing, not federal, to build a railroad across its borders west of the Mississippi. Competition with other cities and states spurred it on to become one of the great hubs of rail transportation in America—these maps are representative of that heritage.

[Fig. a]

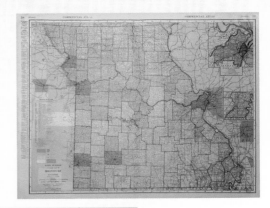

[Fig. b]

[Fig. c]

[Fig. d]

[Fig. e]

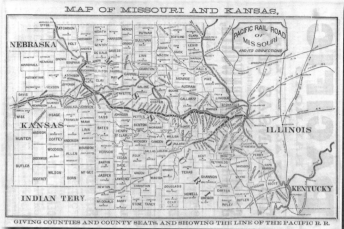

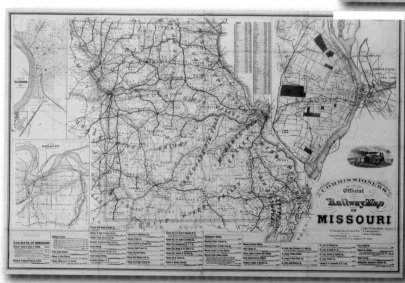

36

Transportaion Map of Missouri. St. Louis: The Missouri Commission, Louisiana Purchase Exposition, 1904 **[36a]**. With *"Kenyon's Highway Map of Missouri"*. Des Moines: Kenyon Co., 1916 roll map **[36 b]**. Also with the *"Rand McNally Auto Trails Map of Missouri"*. 1923 **[Fig. a]**, and the *"American Automobile Association Map of Missouri"*. 1935 **[Fig. b]**.

All *railroads* seemed to lead to the St. Louis World's Fair in 1904 but quickly the need to delineate the growing road system surrounding and encompassing the US Highway system, prominently US 40 and US 66, became very apparent in a new era of readable, accurate and stunning road maps. Missouri became a center for tourism almost from the beginning as Americans took to the highway.

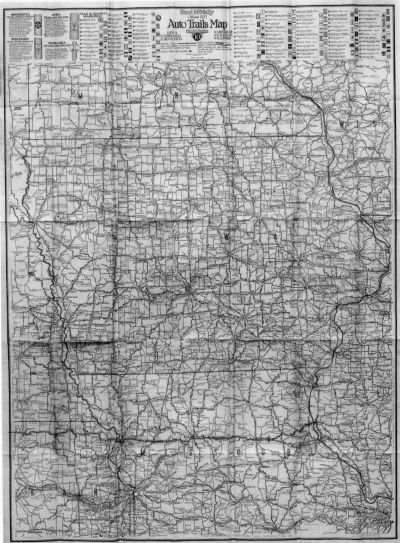

[Fig. a]

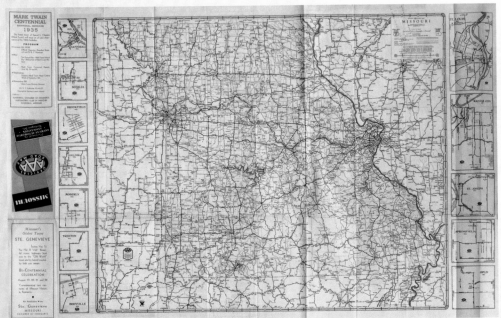

[Fig. b]

[36a]

[36b]

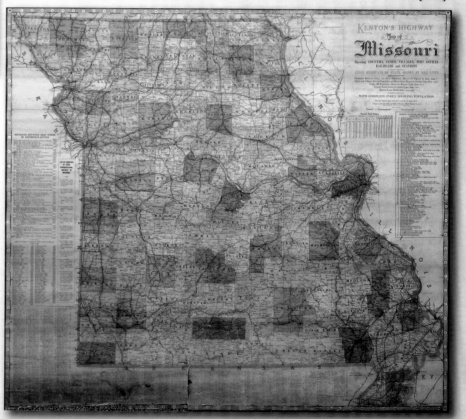

37

D. W. Wellman. *Map of the Missouri River from Surveys Made in Accordance with Acts of Congress Approved June 18, 1878 and March 3, 1879. Index Plate I.* [37]

A monumental work of the river's confluence, giving Missouri its name. A thorough achievement across Missouri, Nebraska and Iowa on a scale of 1 inch to a mile this map charted the namesake of the state and represents well an entire subgenre of great American charts of the river system published for generations.

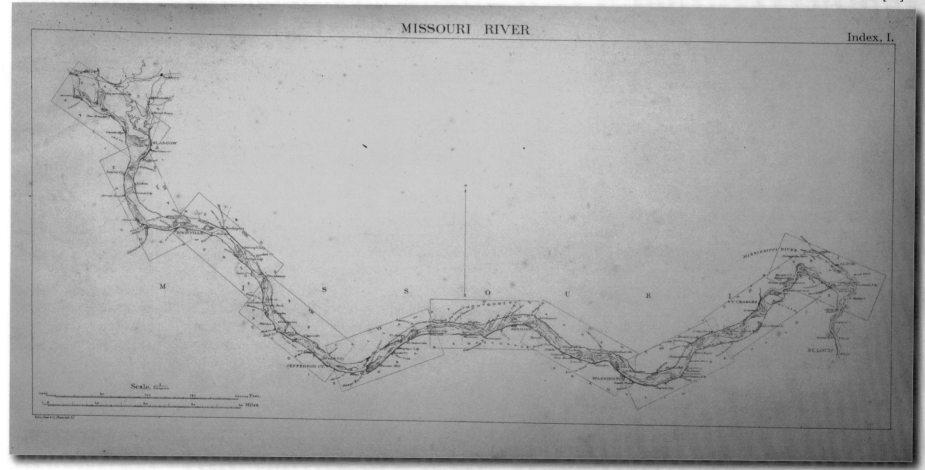

Part Three:

The Transfiguration of St. Louis from a French Colonial Village to an Early American Metropolis; Survivals, Traditions and Change.

[Fig. a]

[Fig. b]

The formative decades of St. Louis occurred without much town planning in the conscious sense. Clearly the site was good, plenty of water and fields and defensible high ground. But there was a subconscious development involved in planning this town which has influenced the grid of the city streets to the present day. Laid out on a model repeated throughout France and New France, removed now from the gentile streams of the Old World for working towns on vast and wide torrents like the St. Lawrence and the Mississippi, there were modifications—these were uncertain frontier cities at first—but the idea of the center market, the common fields, the administrative posts are all with St. Louis from the outset and left an indelible mark on village and city alike.

With two early American atlases comparing the size and plan of **[Fig a]**: *"St. Louis and New Orleans"* and **[Fig b]**: *"St. Louis and Chicago"*; with various plans showing growth of the city (Wayman drawings for 1780, 1796, 1804, 1822, 1841 **[Figs. c, d, e, f, g]** and undated and unsigned *"Map Showing the Boundaries of St. Louis at Different Periods: 1780, 1822, 1839, 1841, 1855, 1860, 1879, and 1876 to 1876"* **[Fig. h]**; with deposition copy map of Chouteau's plan of the village of St. Louis, 1780, ca. 1845, (Courtesy of the Missouri History Museum) **[Fig. i]**; and a plan drawn up by the City Plan Commission in 1910 *"St. Louis Streets in Relation to the French Town System"* showing the lasting effects of the first plan of the city **[Fig. j]**.

[Fig. c]

St. Louis des Illinois
Village in 1780

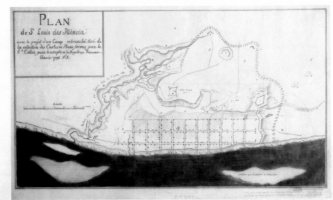
[Fig. d]

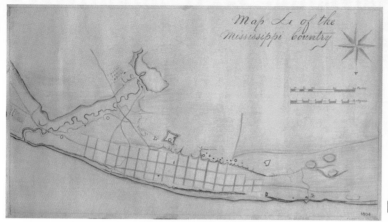

[Fig. e]

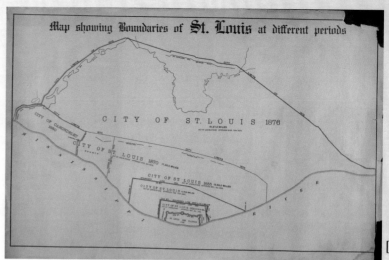

[Fig. h]

[Fig. f]

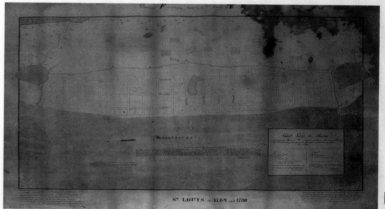

[Fig. i]

Missouri History Museum

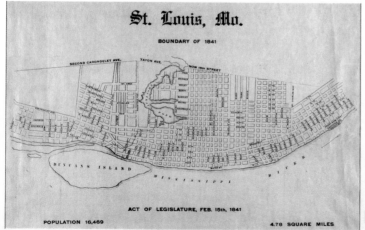

[Fig. g]

[Fig. j]

Plat of the Town of St. Louis with all the Houses on March 10, 1804. A copy drawn by Norbury Waymon of an earlier plat drawn by Frederick Billon **[38]**; and with an early view of St. Louis from 1817, printed originally on a St. Louis bank note **[Fig. a]**; a view of the 1819 village church lot for the earliest Catholic Church built in St. Louis with details of the Bishop's house, the rectory and the stables and gardens prepared in 1850 by Julius Hutawa **[Fig. b]**; and *An Account of Louisiana*. (Philadelphia: Palmer, 1803) usually attributed to Thomas Jefferson as compiler, with the appendix showing the early population records of the Illinois Country as of 1799 **[Fig. c]**.

Billon did not arrive in St. Louis until 1818 with his family and many of the original records and maps of the beginning of the nineteenth century are copies and conjectures, but the city was fortunate to have a citizen like Billon, who became a business leader and a town official, but more importantly, through his status, an early antiquarian and historian for the burgeoning town, which he loved all his life. The plats are remarkable constructions for the earliest days of an active city, one with strong foundations, settled families building a dynastic heritage in St. Louis, banks, docks, churches, estates, newspapers, productive farms, and a fine street (old Market), a causeway to the lifeblood of the river front.

[Fig. a] Eric P. Newman Numismatic Education Society

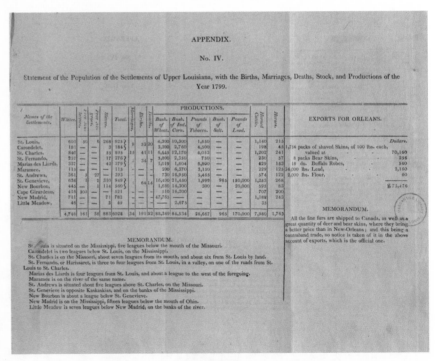

[Fig. c]

[Fig. b]

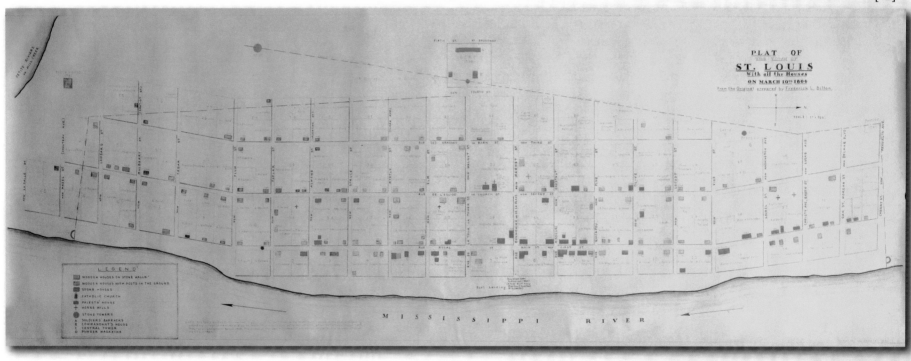

39 Lewis Caleb Beck. *Plan of St. Louis in 1822.* From *A Gazetteer of Illinois and Missouri. Albany: Webster, 1823* **[39a]** with copy enlarged and drawn by Norbury Wayman **[39b]**; with John Melish's map of "St. Louis and adjacent Country" from *A Geographical Description of the United States.* (Philadelphia:1822) **[Fig. a]**.

Beck came to St. Louis briefly and practiced medicine. Returning to New York he produced a series of guides and gazetteer information, including this first for Illinois and Missouri. Melish accompanied his map of the region of St. Louis at the same time with glowing words for the city, the largest west of the Mississippi, with a reported census of 5000 inhabitants and 550 houses, "of which a great proportion were well constructed buildings of brick and stone." He reported that St. Louis, "Standing near the confluence of such mighty streams, the produce of an almost immeasurable extent of back country must flow into it, and that country must be supplied from it, with merchandise."

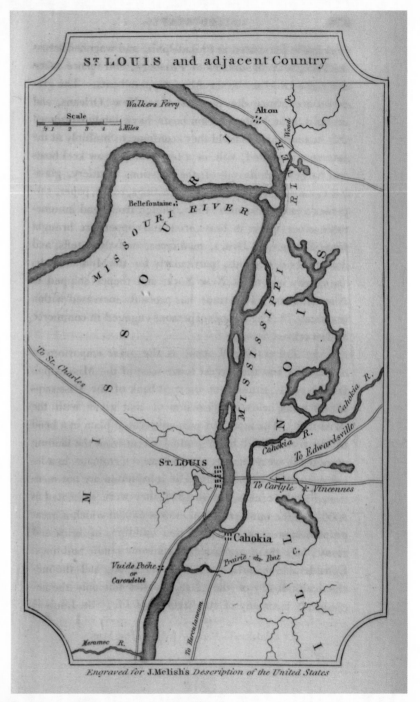

[Fig. a]

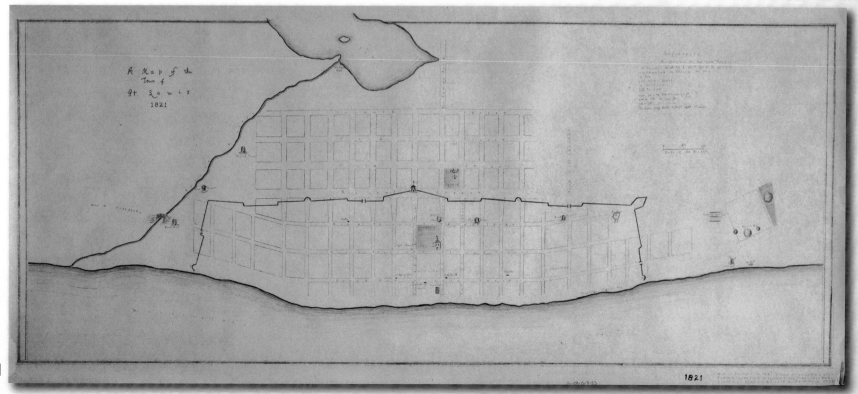

40 Zadok Cramer. ***Map of the Mississippi from St. Louis to the Marameck River (Inserted extra leaf).*** *The Navigator, Containing Directions for Navigating the Monongahela, Allegheny, Ohio, and Mississippi Rivers.* Pittsburgh: Cramer, Spear and Eichbaum, 1811 **[40a]**; with "Mississippi River No. 1". *Reconnaissance of the Mississippi and Ohio Rivers, made during the months of October, November, & December, 1821 by H. Young, W. T. Poussin and S. Tuttle made under the direction of the Board of Engineers* **[40b]**; with Samuel Cumings' "Map Number 1 of the Mississippi River" from *The Western Pilot, containing Charts of the Ohio River and of the Mississippi from the Mouth of the Missouri to the Gulf of Mexico.* Cincinnati: Morgan, Lodge and Fisher, 1825 **[Fig.a]**.

In the time of the flatboats and the coming of the first steamboats documented so well through the early American navigational river guides, maps clearly indicated a future problem for St. Louis and its highly praised river harbor—the city was essentially on a peninsula which could become a remote island due to floods and other naturally occurring circumstances over time. The many islands and sand bars in the river were alarming testament in these early maps.

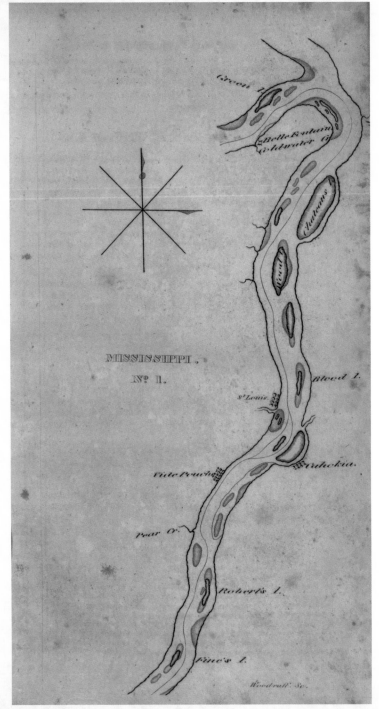

[Fig. a]

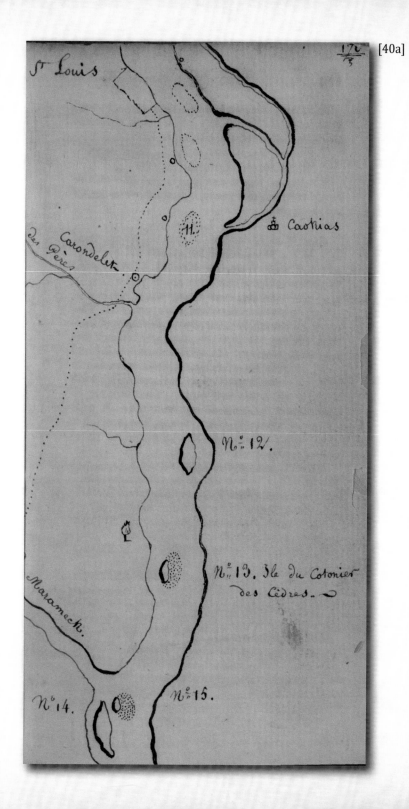

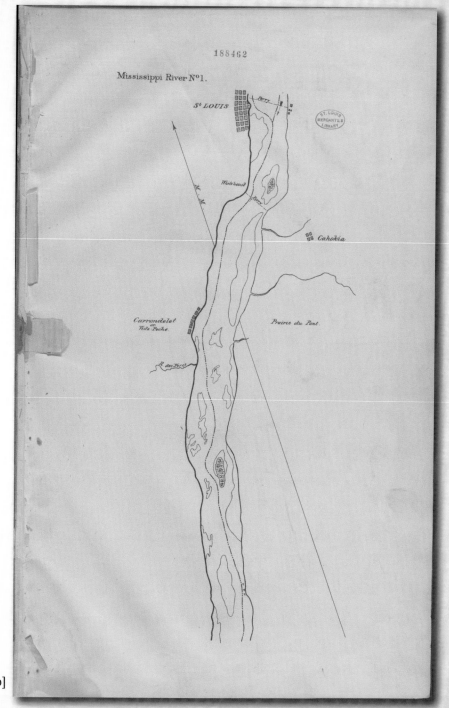

Flood at St. Louis, June 10, 1858.

41 Robert E. Lee. *Map of the Harbor of St. Louis; Mississippi River.* Washington, D.C.: W.J. Stone, 1837 **[41]**.

The young Lt. Lee arrived in St. Louis in the city's first booming days, a heady time that was not sustainable due to the growing sandbars and river islands which began to limit access to the city's levees, imperiling the entire economy based on river trade and traffic. Lee and German-born engineer, Henry Kayser, devised a series of underwater jetties depicted on this important and highly detailed map, intended to divert stronger river currents toward the St. Louis side of the river; the project was not fully completed before it was successfully proved to have saved the harbor. Lee received several promotions in the army engineering work he would oversee along the Mississippi.

St. Louis Levee, 1850.

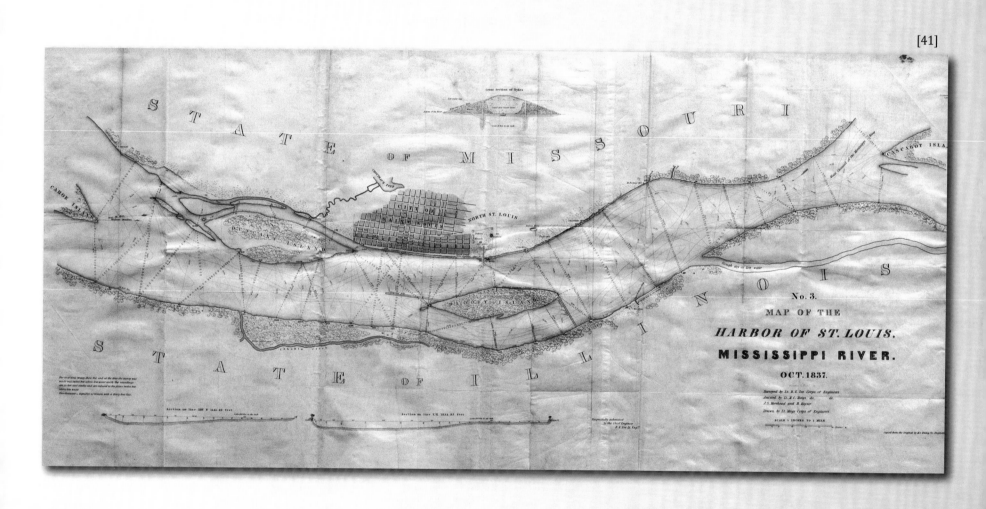

No. 3.

MAP OF THE

HARBOR OF ST. LOUIS,

MISSISSIPPI RIVER.

OCT. 1837.

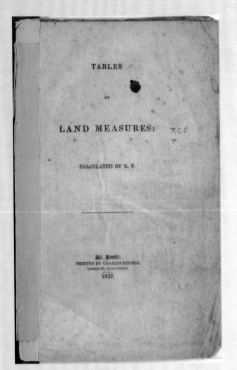

[Fig. a]

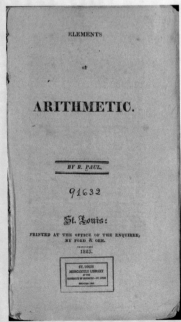

[Fig. c]

South St. Louis.

A NUMBER OF

Valuable Lots

IN SOUTH ST. LOUIS.

WILL BE SOLD BY

FRANKLIN & JENKINS.

At their Auction Room, 15 Broad-street.

ON TUESDAY 24th JANUARY,

1837.

AT TWELVE O'CLOCK.

NEW-YORK.

W. APPLEGATE, PRINTER,

261, Hudson-street.

[Fig. b]

42 Rene Paul. ***Plan of the City of Saint Louis, Survey Ordered July 10n 1823, Completed in December, 1823, Adopted in March, 1824; Revised and Corrected in June, 1835,*** manuscript copy for official business **[42a]**; with printed version of the same referenced plan and map, facsimile, 1968 **[42 b]**; and with Eugene C. Dupre's *"Map of the St. Louis Common Fields, Township 45 North, Range 7 East"* (St. Louis, 1838) **[42c]**; with *Tables of Land Measures, Calculated by R.P.* (Rene Paul). St. Louis: Keemle, 1837 **[Fig. a]**; and a prospectus for the sale of "South St. Louis, Valuable Lots"in 1837 **[Fig. b]**; and Rene Paul's *Elements of Arithmetic* (St. Louis; Ford, 1823) **[Fig. c]**.

The first official city maps of St. Louis were surveyed by its first official engineer and reflect the evolution of the trading post into a full service city and community, with needs for residents, travelers and visitors of all types. His work as a city engineer in the 1820s and 1830s indicates the city's growing prominence in the Middle West after nearly seventy five years as a colonial outpost for the fur trading special interest upon which it was founded. Paul came to St. Louis from the Napoleonic wars. He became a business associate of Pierre Chouteau and married into the Chouteau family, and through these connections built a professional career in St. Louis as a respected surveyor from 1823-1838. He taught mathematics in St. Louis' first college and wrote *Elements of Arithmetic* the first textbook published west of the Mississippi. Most likely his calculation tables hold a printing record as well for an early technical reference. In the 1830s seemingly everyone wanted a print or view of the new town or a map of property; Eugene Dupre was an entrepreneur, first coming to St. Louis as a tailor, next a lithographer and mapmaker in these busy days for the city.

[42a]

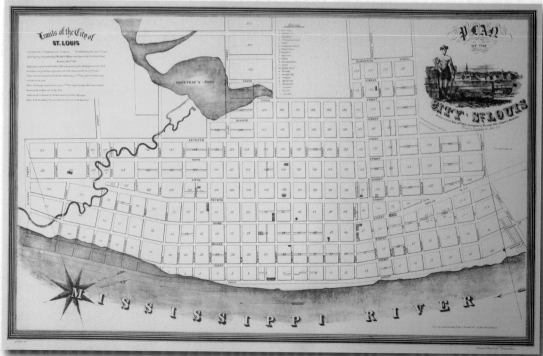

[42b]

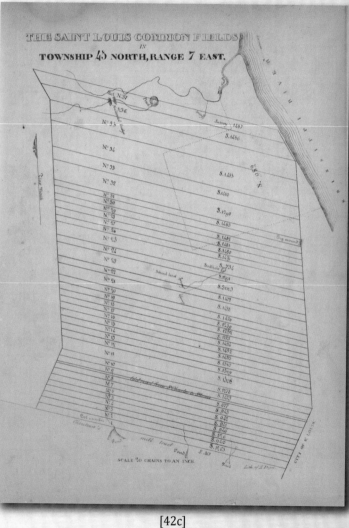

[42c]

43

Julius Hutawa. ***Fracl. Township 45 N. R. 7 E.*** From *Atlas of the County of St. Louis, Missouri by Congressional Townships compiled by Edward Hutawa.* (*St. Louis: Hutawa, 1848*) **[43a]**; with *Sectional Map of the County of St. Louis, Missouri, St. Louis: Julius Hutawa, 1848* **[43b]**; and with Hutawa's *Map of the City of St. Louis* accompanying W. D. Skillman's *The Western Metropolis, or St. Louis in 1846.* (St. Louis: Skillman, 1846) **[Fig. a]**; and James M. Kershaw's *Map and View of St. Louis,* appearing in Sloss' *The St. Louis Directory for 1848 (St. Louis: Charles and Hammond, 1848)* **[43c]**.

Hutawa came to St. Louis from eastern Europe in the early 1830s with family members and settled in St. Louis, a home base for a lithography business which lasted for many years and which specialized in maps—some of the very first west of the Mississippi for an American city of any kind—and of the American west. Skillman's almanac in the important year of 1846 depict St. Louis at a crossroads period but with a look back and serves as one of the early histories of St. Louis. Kershaw's plans shows in the border the great building occurring in St. Louis in the 1840s, truly a frontier metropolis in the making.

[43a]

TOWNSHIP 45 NORTH, RANGE 7 EAST
Confirmed Claims

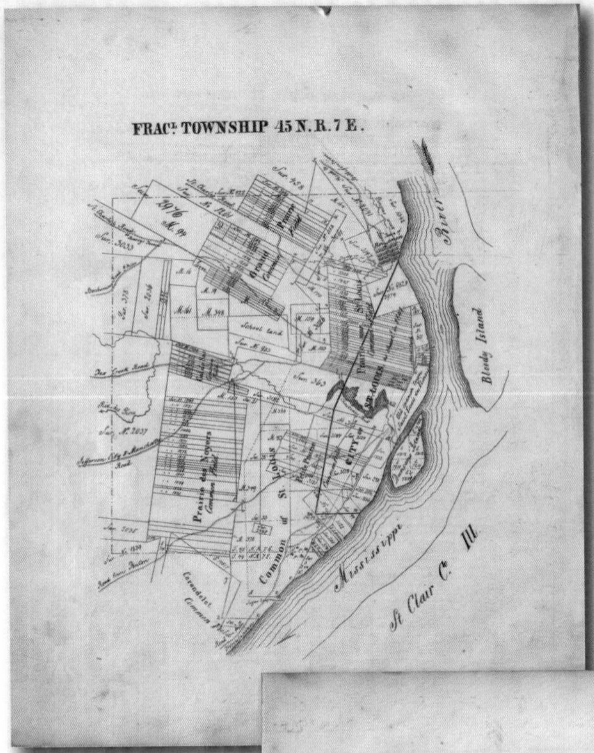

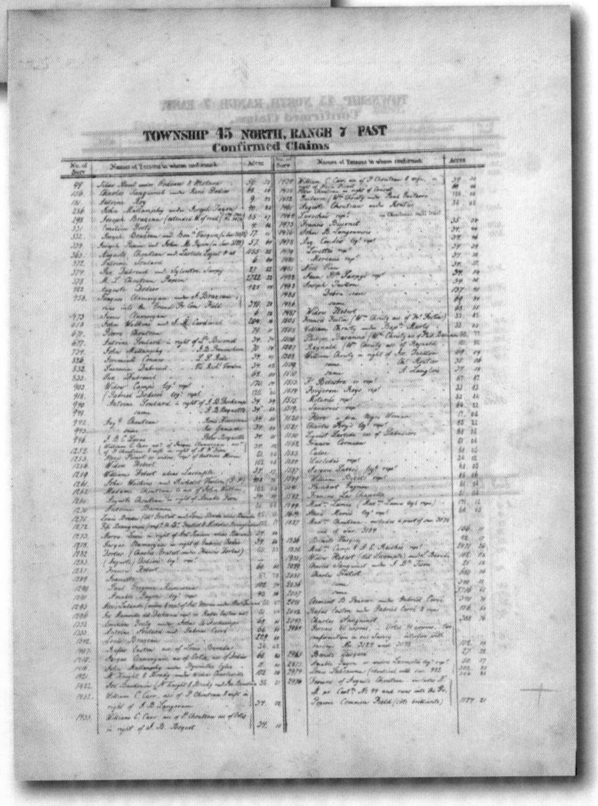

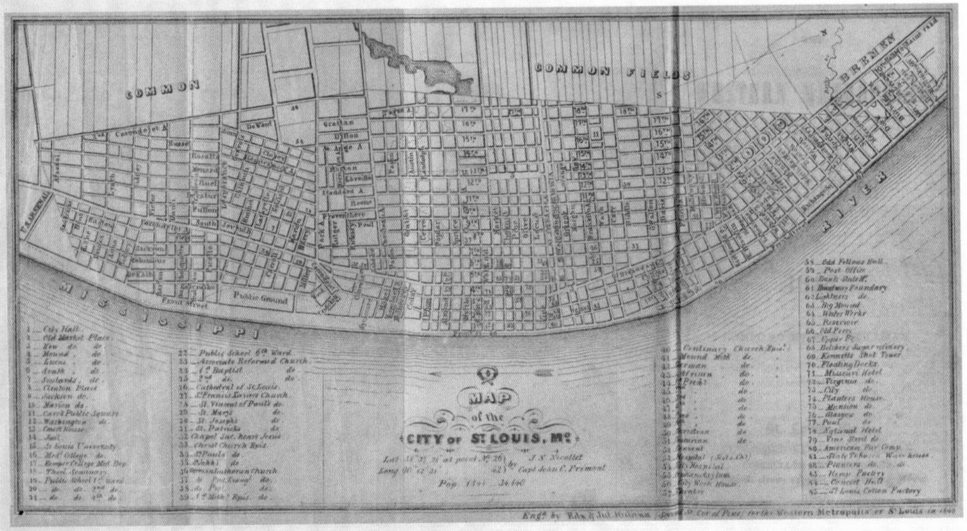

[Fig. a]

[43b]

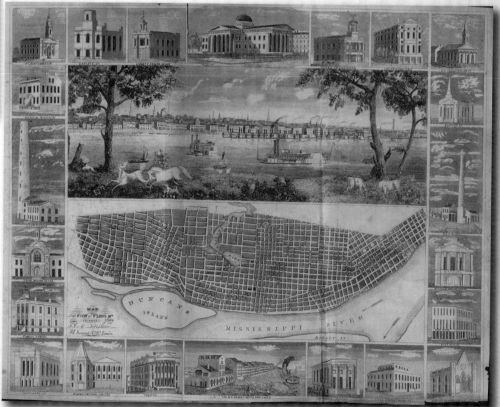

[43c]

93

44 Julius Hutawa. *Plan of the City of St. Louis.* St. Louis: Hutawa and Gast, 1850 **[44]**.

A tour de force plan perfectly integrated with a view of the city viewed straight ahead at eye level in alignment with the map.

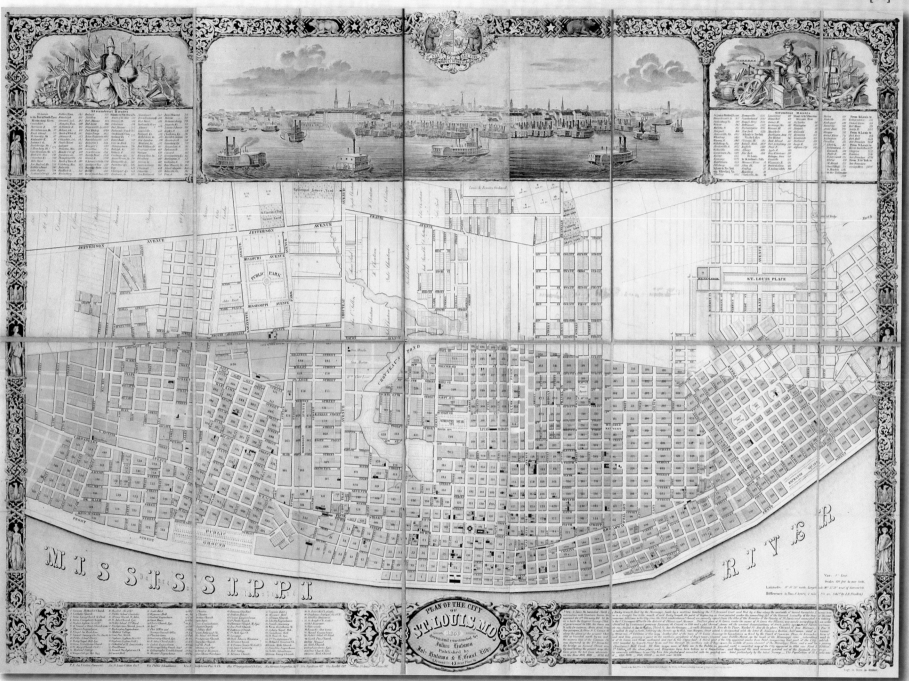

45 Julius Hutawa. *Map of the City of St. Louis, Mo.* St. Louis: Hutawa, 1851 **[45a]**; with Morrison's *St. Louis City Directory for 1852*, including a version of this map without elaboration **[Fig. a]**; with Green's *St. Louis Directory for 1851, including a detail of the business district for an advertisement to "Corinthian Hall"* **[Fig. b]**; and with Hutawa's *"Map of the United States Shewing the Principal Steamboat Routes and Projected Railroads Connecting with St. Louis".* (*St. Louis: Mo. Republican, 1854*) **[45b]**; and Hutawa's *"Map Shewing the Experimental Lines Surveyed during the Summer of 1850 from St. Louis to the Western Line of the State of Missouri for the Pacific Rail Road"* accompanying *First Annual Report of the Board of Directors of the Pacific Railroad and the Report of the Chief Engineer upon the Preliminary Surveys. St. Louis: Republican, 1851* **[Fig. c]**; with *"Kennedy's Sectional Map of St. Louis with Street Directory"* in R. V. Kennedy's *St. Louis Directory, 1859.* (*St. Louis: Alex. McLean, 1859*) **[45c]**; and J.H. Fisher's *"Map of the City of St. Louis, Mo. and Vicinity",* 1853 in History, Abstracts of Title, Evidences of Location, &c. Relating to the Common Field Lots of the South Grand Prairie and Cul de Sac of the Grand Prairie and an Argument in Support of Cozen's Survey by Henry Williams. (St. Louis: Mo. Republican Office, 1854) **[Fig. d]**; and **[Fig. e]**, a plat map of an 1854 land argument, *"The Chauvin Claim"* and **[Fig. f]**: *"The City of St. Louis",* an 1855 map published by J. H. Colton in New York in 1855 with **[Fig. g]**: *D. B. Cooke's Railway Guide for Illinois Showing all the Stations with their Respective Distances Connecting with Chicago, (Chicago: Cooke, 1855).*

The busy town of St. Louis was mapping and arguing about land claims as it prepared for the coming of the iron horse—everyone was talking about that and these maps are all related and show an engagement with preparing for economic boom; yet the 1855 map of Illinois, the growing giant to the east, relates a severe competitive mentality.

[Fig. b]

[Fig. c]

[Fig. d]

[Fig. a]

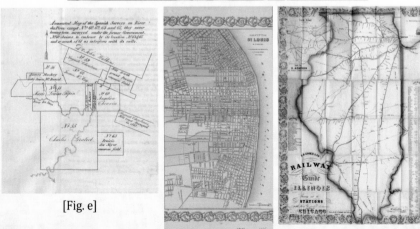

[Fig. e]

[Fig. f]

[Fig. g]

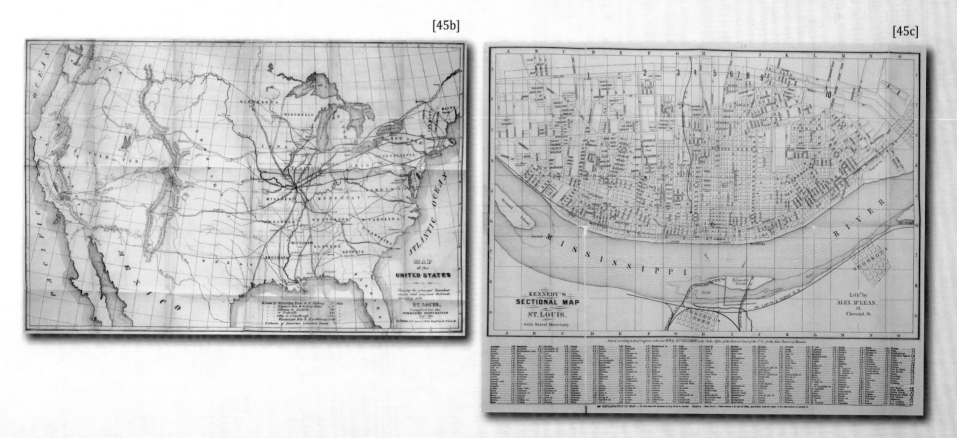

46

F. H. Gerdes. *Comparative Map of the Shore Line of the Mississippi River in front of St. Louis, Missouri, Prepared by Order of Rear Admiral C.H. Davis U.S.N. Chairman of the U.S. Commission for a Naval Site in the Western Waters.* Washington, 1865. **[46a]**; with a plan of Camp Jackson, 1861 by Edward B. Sayers **[46b]**; four maps of St. Louis in the late 1860s: The 1867 map of S. A. Mitchell **[Fig. a]**; Mclean's *"Sectional Map of St. Louis"* appearing in *Stranger's Guide to St. Louis, or What to See and How to See It. (St. Louis: Winter, 1867)* **[Fig. b]**; and Theodore Fay's *"Guide Map to the City of St. Louis" (St. Louis: Cook, 1867)* **[Fig. c]**; and a copy by Norbury Wayman of L. J. Zwanziger's 1867 *"Map of the City of St. Louis"*, published by Theodore Schrader **[Fig. d]**; and William H. Merrill's *"Harbor of St. Louis. 1869"* taken from Mayor's published *Message* of the same year **[Fig. e]**.

The 1860s in St. Louis was a time for strategy with military operations abounding in and around the city at the beginning, continued growth of a major urban landscape after the worst years of the war, and further concerns to understand the natural blessings and challenges of the great harbor confluence. Davis' plan for a naval base presented in a Senate Document (38th Congress) is indicative of the strategic importance of the Harbor of St. Louis in the uncertain days of the Lower Mississippi blockades leading to the naval engagements at Memphis and Vicksburg. After the war these 1867 maps show St. Louis as a destination, a place to be for business and settlement. Building was unabated in the war years, a dangerous time for a city virtually under martial law and refugee camp for persons of the most divided viewpoint. The Camp Jackson plan is a remarkable survival taken down by a Missouri surveyor who served eventually as an engineer in the Confederate Army, and he documents the battle plan near St. Louis University of one of the earliest battles of the Civil War virtually in the new streets of St. Louis.

[Fig. a]

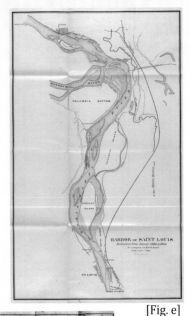

[Fig. e]

[Fig. b]

[Fig. c]

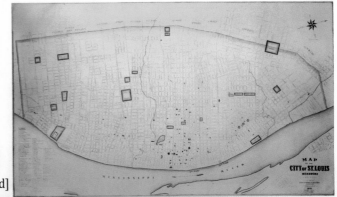

[Fig. d]

№ 1.

References relative to Harbor Improvements

COMPARATIVE MAP
of the shore line of the
MISSISSIPPI RIVER
in front of
ST. LOUIS, MISSOURI
Prepared by order of Rear Admiral C.H. Davis U.S.N.
Chairman of the U.S. Commission for a Naval Site
in the Western Waters.
By the Coast Survey Party of
F.H. Gerdes U.S.C.S. Topl. Engr. to the Commission
Compiled from surveys made from 1861 to 1862.

SCALE OF FEET

CARONDELET

CABARET ID.

CAHOKIA BAY

ARSENAL ISLAND

KERR'S ISLAND

DUNCAN'S ID.

BLOODY ID.

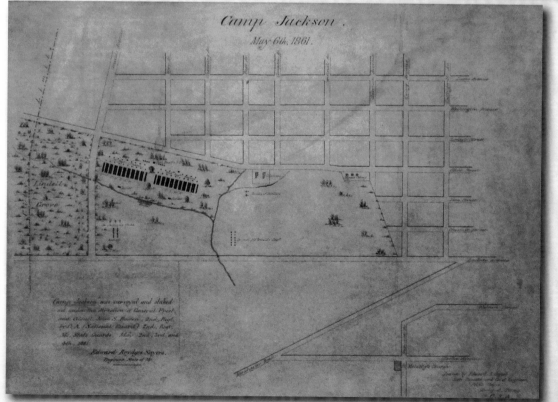

Camp Jackson.
May 6th, 1861.

47 C. T. Uhlmann. *Township Map 43, Range 7 East, Showing Jefferson Barracks* in *Atlas of the County of St. Louis*, Missouri. St. Louis, Julius Hutawa, 1862. **[47]**

This massive atlas survey of St. Louis, undertaken at the height of the Civil War, was given to the St. Louis Mercantile Library by the County Clerk as inscribed April 28, 1863.

William A. Mosberger. ***Ross' New Map of the City of St. Louis; A Complete Stranger's Guide Showing all the Prominent Buildings, Parks, Streets, Street Railways &c.*** St. Louis: E. H. Ross, 1871 **[48]**; with other city maps from the 1870s: two maps by Julius Hutawa, the first from De Yongh's 1871-2 *Business Directory*, the second from J. L. Tracy's *Guide to Missouri and St. Louis*, 1871 **[Fig. a and Fig. b]**; with a similar map from the Westbrook, Edwards and Sage's *St. Louis Commercial Directory*, 1873 **[Fig. c]** with two 1872 maps of St. Louis from popular contemporary atlases **[Fig. d, e]**.

Mosberger was a talented surveyor who worked in a typically excellent firm with Ross and Alexander McLean on many Midwestern state and city projects; this was a time when St. Louis map publishing was highly regarded and sought after.

[Fig. a]

[Fig. c]

[Fig. b]

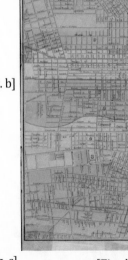

[Fig. d]

[Fig. e]

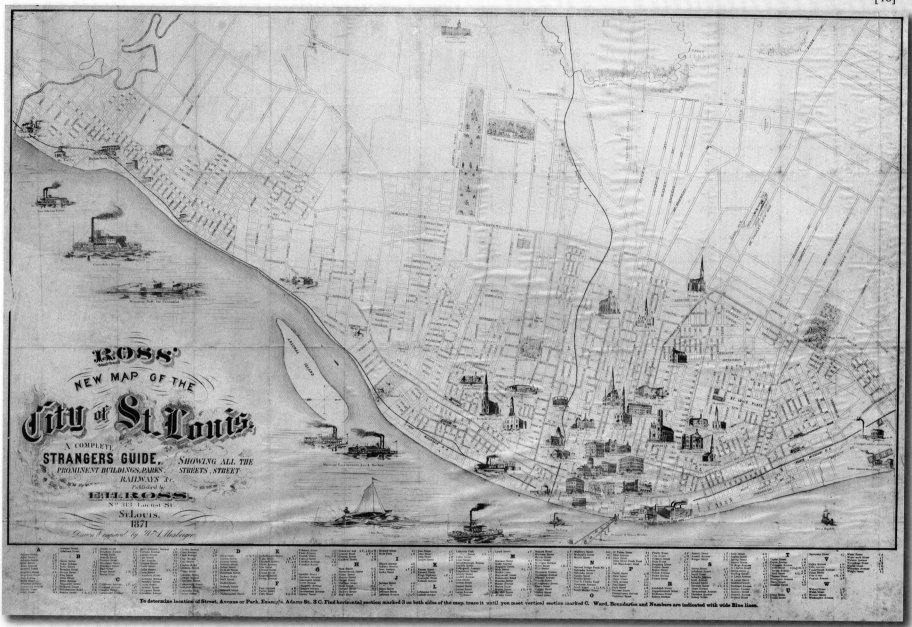

49

L. U. Reavis. *A Map Illustrative of the Continental Argument in Favor of St. Louis Becoming the Future Great City of the World.* St. Louis: Tribune Publishing Co., 1874 **[49]**.

Published in one of Reavis' many works of civic promotion, *St. Louis; the Commercial Metropolis of the Mississippi Valley*, this map does not seem less visionary than the very serious national debate to move the federal capital to St. Louis, which actually occured at this time. This map shows the outlook of St. Louis, based on an age old understanding of the geopolitics in the center of the continent.

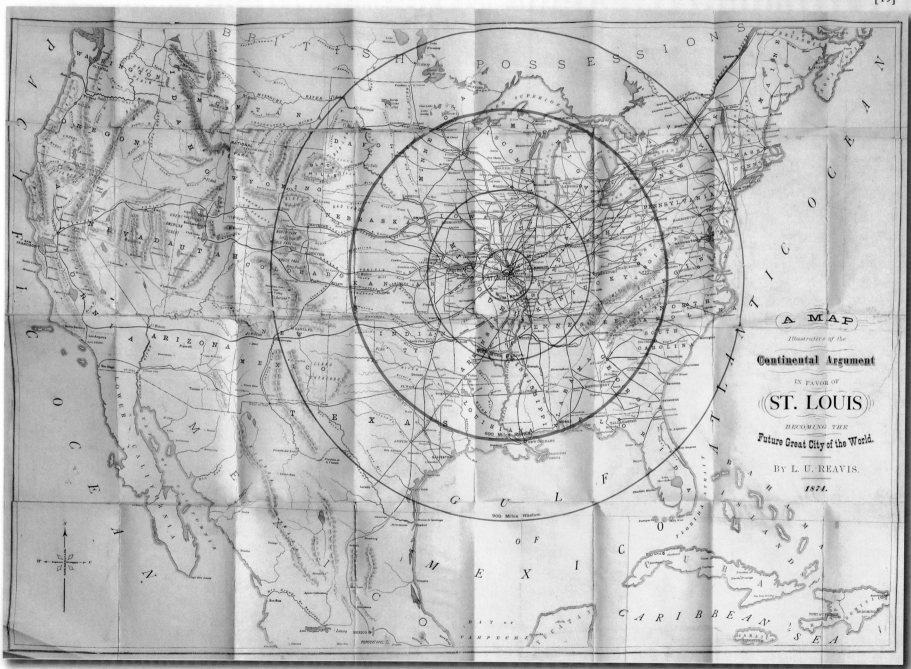

A MAP

Illustrative of the

Continental Argument

IN FAVOR OF

ST. LOUIS

BECOMING THE

Future Great City of the World.

BY L. U. REAVIS.

1874.

The Compton and Dry Atlas:

A City Bounded to its Fullest Extent and yet Boundless.

In the 1870s the great American tradition of bird's eye views became a popular way of depicting the seemingly limitless potential and growth of the great American cities. St. Louis was no exception and several documented the city's prominence in this period, none more typical than C. K. Lord's *"View of St. Louis and Vicinity"* (St. Louis, 1876) **[Fig. a]**; or Parsons and Atwater's *"View of St. Louis"* published by Nathaniel Currier and James Ives (New York, 1874) **[Fig. b]**. These large scale views gave an encyclopedic picture of their urban subject, as much a guide to a visitor as a travelogue to the armchair visitor.

[Fig. a]

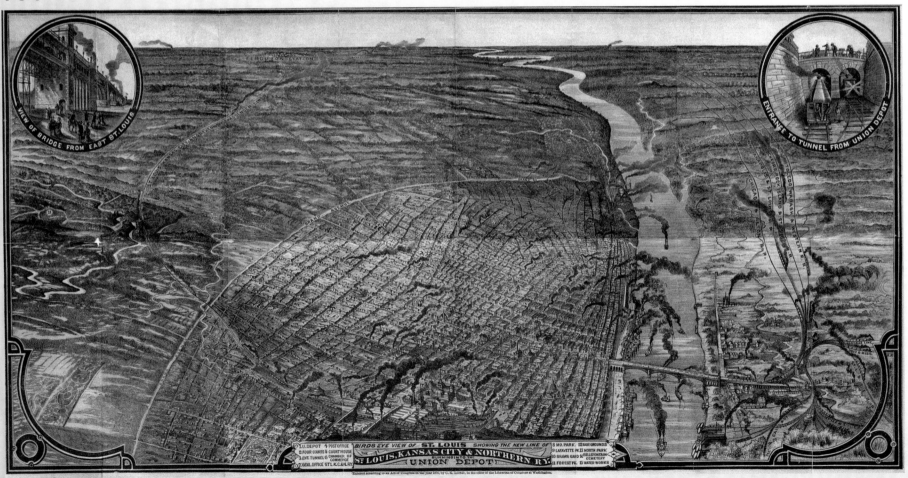

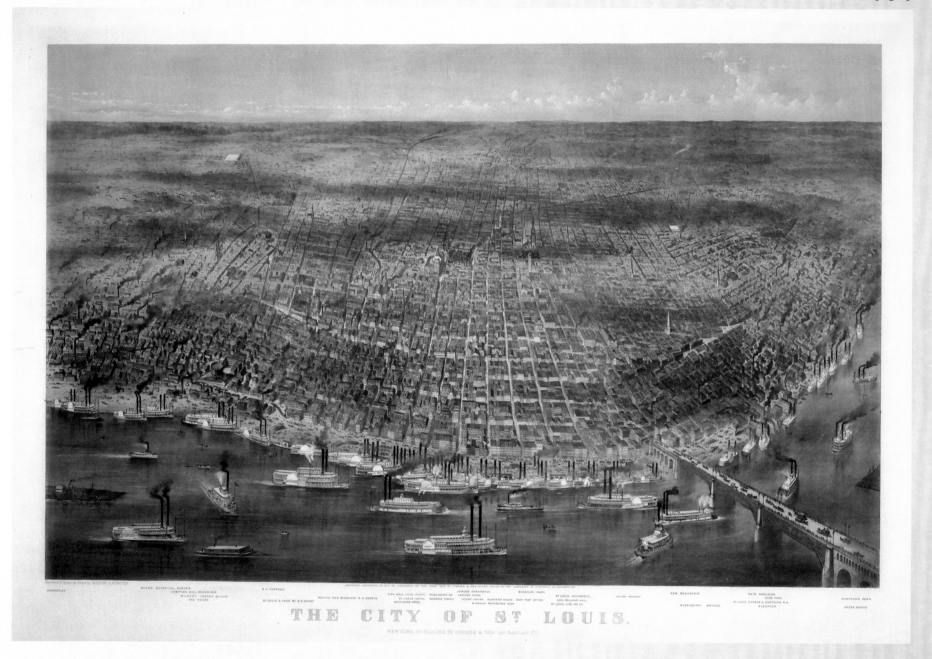

THE CITY OF ST. LOUIS.

50

Camille N. Dry and Richard J. Compton. *Pictorial St. Louis; the Great Metropolis of the Mississippi Valley: A Topographical Survey Drawn in Perspective A.D. 1875.* St. Louis: Compton and Company, 1875 [50a]; Plate of *Key to the Perspective with map of the territory in the Perspective*; [Fig. a]; Plates 1, 2, 21 and 22 of the riverfront of St. Louis [Fig. b]; [Fig. c]; [Fig. d]; [Fig. e]; Plate 5 [50b]; Plate 43 [50c] the current St. Louis University area and near old Camp Jackson, (see plan item 46b); Plates 59 and 62 [50d]; [50e] show bucolic town and country.

Many of the best surveyors, mapmakers and printers in St. Louis worked on this massive document of the several thousand square miles of 1870s St. Louis. This survey was one of the most ambitious ever attempted for an American city and showed the fullest application of the day for lithographic printing. The Compton and Dry plates form a huge picture of St. Louis before its boundary was set to the present day—it showed nearly limitless growth potential in the dense city limits and the vistas of St. Louis County presented one pastoral setting after another. In this time county atlases were very popular and to some extent, the Compton and Dry atlas is the parent of them all, nothing ever approached it. The Mercantile Library is grateful to Mr. Blackford F. Brauer for allowing the loan of an additional set of loose plates from a disbound volume in order to form a continuous view of the Compton and Dry panoramic perspective, as framed for this exhibition from these 110 individual plates.

[Fig. b]

[Fig. c]

[Fig. d]

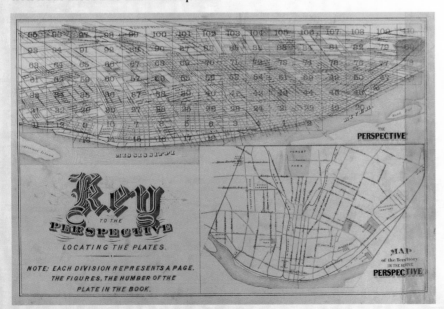

[Fig. a]

[Fig. e]

[50a]

[50b]

[50c]

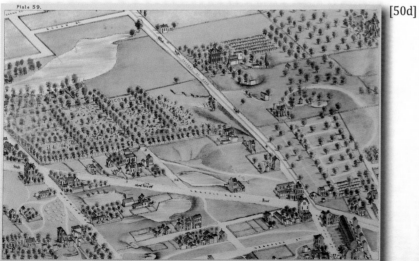
[50d]

[50e]

109

Part Four:

St. Louis, "The Fourth City"; An Industrial Giant and Beyond

51

Central Township Map of St. Louis County. (1878) **[51a]**; with a copy of the *Scheme for the Separation and Re-Organization of the Governments of St. Louis City and County, and Charter for the City of Saint Louis. (St. Louis: Woodward, Tiernan &Hale, 1877)* **[51b]**.

Perhaps one of the most important printed documents for St. Louis history, on the binding was proclaimed the "Charter of the City of St. Louis, Adopted by the People, 1876" after years of complaining about taxation problems, corruption, political wrangling and voter fraud. This document did not change the face of the city map-wise and much as it froze it in time; new municipalities, always truly part of a cohesive urban area, popped up around the city limits in a way that was indistinguishable from the city itself to be sure, but that was already apparent in this 1878 plat of the central corridor, even in the Compton and Dry *Atlas*, (see item 50).

Maybe the numbers were juggled a bit on the census leading to the claim that St. Louis at the turn of the century was the third of fourth largest city in America, but these maps show that St. Louis, indeed, was and always has been a very big city, with the benefits and problems of the urban environment. The growth of the city was constantly celebrated and analyzed through charts and maps as a plan of The Physical Growth of St. Louis from 1950 indicates **[Fig. a]**.

[Fig. a]

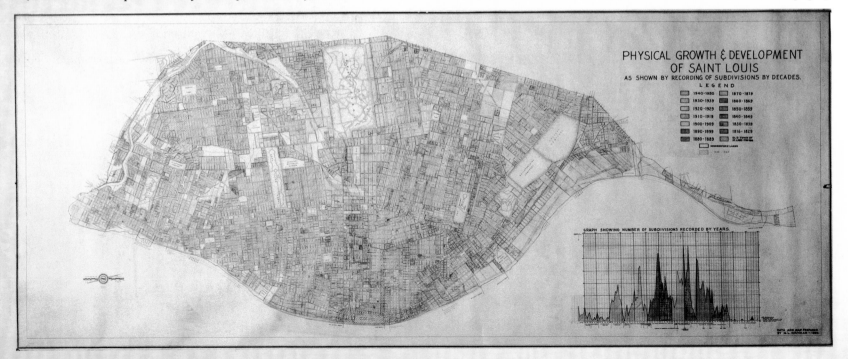

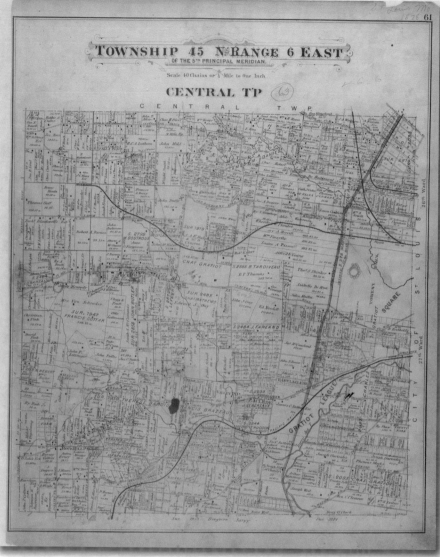

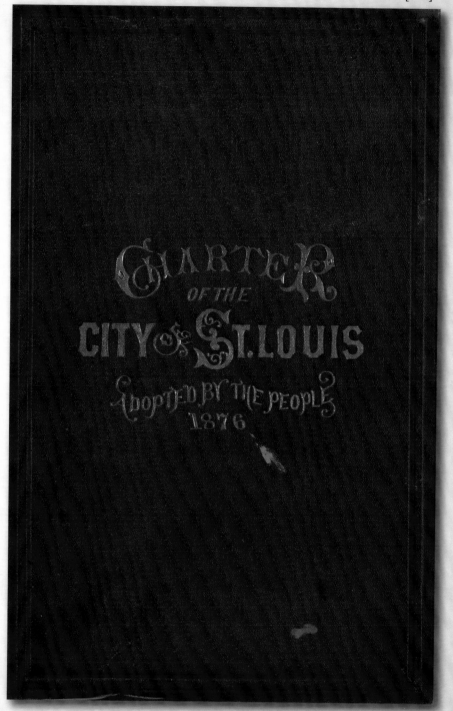

52

G. M. Hopkins. **Map of Forest Park.** Plate 40 in *Atlas of the City of St. Louis.* Philadelphia: 1883 **[52a]**; with *"Map of Saint Louis, Mo., and Suburbs"*, (author and publisher not noted, undated, ca. 1885) **[52b]**; with detail of an 1884 roll "Map of St. Clair County, Ill.", by C. F. Hillgard (Schrader, 1884), with full section on railroad yards in East St. Louis **[52c]**; and with two printings of R. A. Campbell's popular *"Revised Guide Map of St. Louis"* from the early 1880s, both giving way to business advertisements, rather that vignettes of municipal structures **[Fig. a]**; **[Fig. b]**; and with a guidebook of the city's backstreets of this time, written to titillate and ostensibly warn the reader of this period: *Dark and Mysterious Places of St. Louis*; (St. Louis: Olive, 1885) **[Fig. c]**; and two scenes of St. Louis celebratory street processions from **[Figs. d and e]**, from *Rolling-pin's Illustrated Exposition and Street Parades.* (St. Louis: 1886, 1887).

Hopkins was a civil engineer who made some of the earliest detailed property maps for cities like St. Louis, but in a clear and artistic style. From the 1860s to the early 1900s, St. Louis was fortunate to have a group of dedicated atlases like this and, for example, the Compton and Dry masterpiece (see Item 50). The early school map is one of the most detailed for the area in the 1880s. It is of great interest in cataloguing the properties of the St. Louis Public School system. This was a period of living and using the streets for a backdrop and celebrations, from national political conventions to trade fairs and parades and has been thus well documented in the surviving popular press of the time, giving a glimpse of these streets as stage sets.

[Fig. a]

[Fig. b]

[Fig. c]

[Fig. d]

[Fig. e]

Road work in St. Louis.

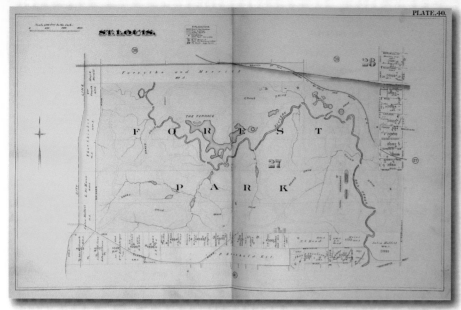

[52a]

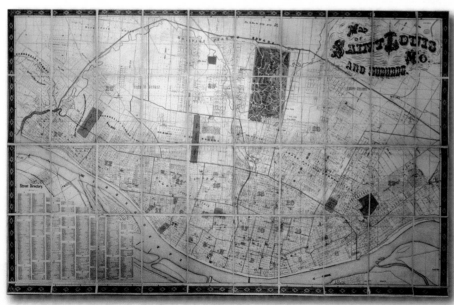

[52b]

[52c]

53

Map of the Properties, and Railway Terminals of the Wiggens Ferry Company. 1897 **[53a]**; with a scene of early St. Louis ferry transport by Leon Pomarede in his "View of St. Louis in 1832" appearing in the Compton and Dry *Pictorial St. Louis* in 1875 **[Fig. a]**; and with Julius Pitzman's plan of the "St. Louis Union Stockyards" (undated, late 19th century) **[53b]**; also with special maps for lighting *(1898)* **[Fig.b]**; sewer drains *(1897)* **[Fig. c]**; elections, *(1898)* **[Fig. d]** and the first consistently paved roads published by the Automobile Club of St. Louis *(1897)* **[Fig. e]** ; with A. C. Shewey's contemporary maps of St. Louis and St. Louis County **[Figs. f and g]**; and Higgins & Company's roll map of St. Louis for 1897 one of the best school and reference maps of the city to it time **[Fig. h]**.

The remarkable map of the Wiggens Company, a ferry and transport company from the early 1790s to well past the 1890s with extensive railroad and bridge interests, shows the extensive east side infrastructure at this time just in getting people and goods to the west shore of the river. Julius Pitzman came to St. Louis after the Civil War and showed great skill and talent in planning, quickly to become the City Surveyor. He helped lay out the plans for Forest Park and numerous other civil works for St. Louis. The St. Louis Union Stockyards in this plan were being modified and brought into coordination as much as anything with the east side's National Stockyards both vital institutions and part of the legendary and historic connection of St. Louis with western and southwestern economics, as with the cattle trade and industry, for generations.

[Fig. c]

[Fig. d]

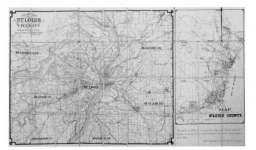

[Fig. e]

[Fig. f]

[Fig. g]

[Fig. a]

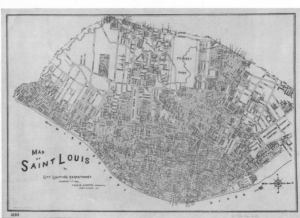

[Fig. b]

[Fig. h]

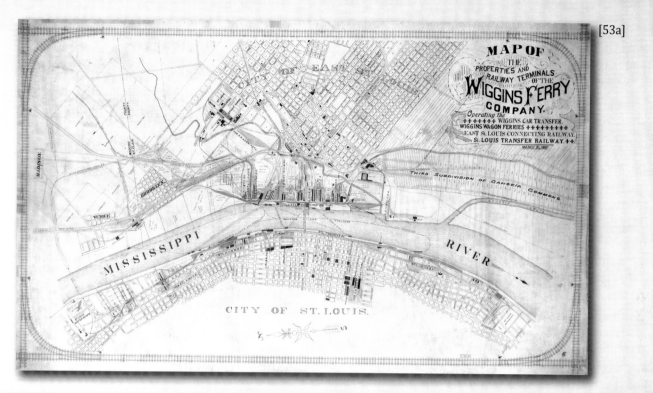

[53a]

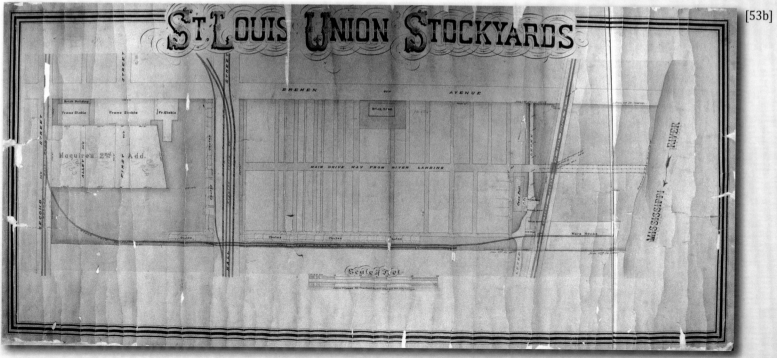

[53b]

54

Ground Plan of the St. Louis World's Fair. Louisiana Purchase Exposition, 1904 **[54a]**; and a contemporary map of St. Louis from the same period published by the Leipzig firm of Wagner and Debes **[Fig. a]**; with the U.S. Geological Survey map by Cooke, Tufts and Young and the City of St. Louis of 1903, published in 1904 and reprinted in 1932 **[54b]**; with two maps from the 1909 *Plat Book of St. Louis County, Missouri* (Des Moines, Northwest Publishing Co.) of **[Fig. b]**: *"St. Louis County"* and **[Fig. c]**: *"West Part of Webster Groves"*, and with three wall maps of St. Louis from 1902 and 1907, the latter published that year for the city and the region by the indefatigable Higgins & Co., proclaimed as the leading "map coloring and engraving specialists" **[Figs. d, e, f]**; *The Election Commissioners Map of St. Louis for the Election of 1904 ("Election Commissioners Political Atlas of St. Louis for 1906"* with ward maps printed by Higgins and Co.) **[Fig. g]**; and with a 1909 Davis Realty Development Co. 1909 *St. Louis map, proclaiming it "The Coming Giant of America".* **[54c]**

It would be easy for a citizen of St. Louis at the turn of the century to prophesy in this way—the metropolis was growing, the suburbs of the county were filling in with population and land was selling briskly. It seemed everyone was coming to St. Louis—meeting in it—at the famous World's Fair. Perhaps the most important maps ever made for the city, showing as much promise and potential as those of the late 1700s and early 1800s in fact, were from this period when the world took note once again of the heart of the Mississippi Valley.

[Fig. e]

[Fig. c]

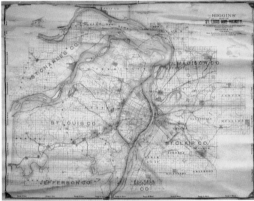

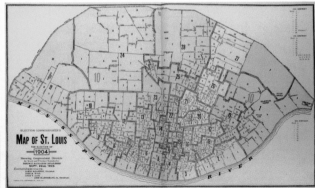

[Fig. f]

[Fig. d]

[Fig. a]

[Fig. b]

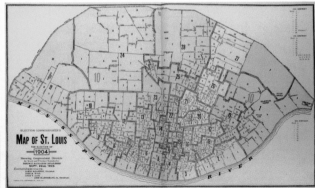

[Fig. g]

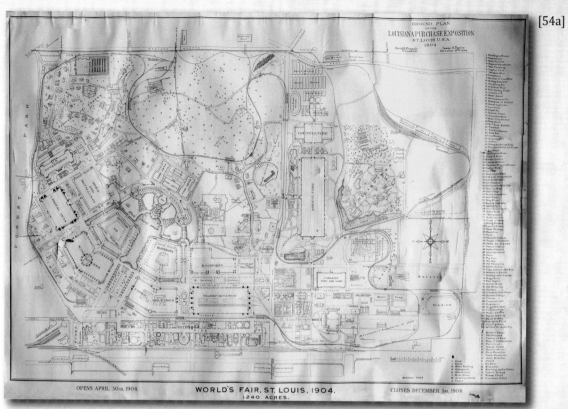

[54a]

[54b]

[54c]

55

Map of the City of St. Louis. St. Louis: O. Schrowang, 1914 **[55a]**; with the Rand McNally "New Commercial Atlas Map of St. Louis" (1912) **[55b]**; and with Automobile Map of St. Louis County, (St. Louis: Charles Hoelscher, 1912) **[Fig. a]**.

St. Louis on the eve of World War One.

New hazards of horseless carriages on old St. Louis boulevards.

[55b]

[55a]

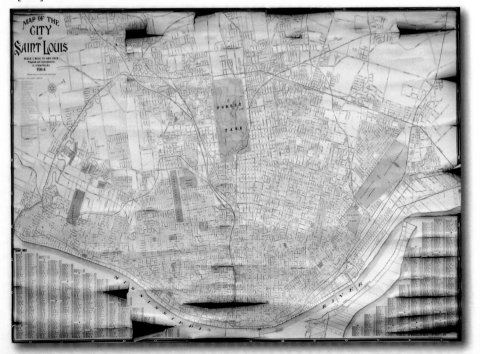

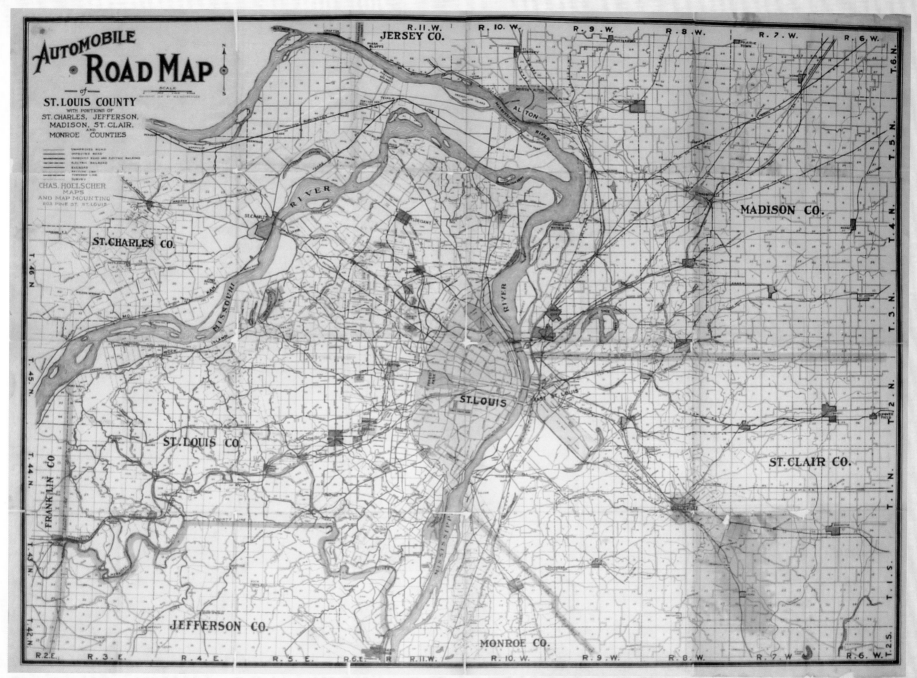

119

Map of Saint Louis and County Adjoining. M. A. Higgins Co., 1912 [56].

One of the largest maps of the city ever published as a single document, an amazing planning map for the use of the commissions beginning to view St. Louis from a "city beautiful" perspective. Land availability, the regional setting, and redevelopment potential are carefully catalogued on this map. The maps of the early years of the century for St. Louis begin to document more thoroughly the regional environment, leaving the city's riverfront as more a back door or a working entrance, rather than as the destination it had always previously been considered.

Washington Ave. at Broadway looking north.

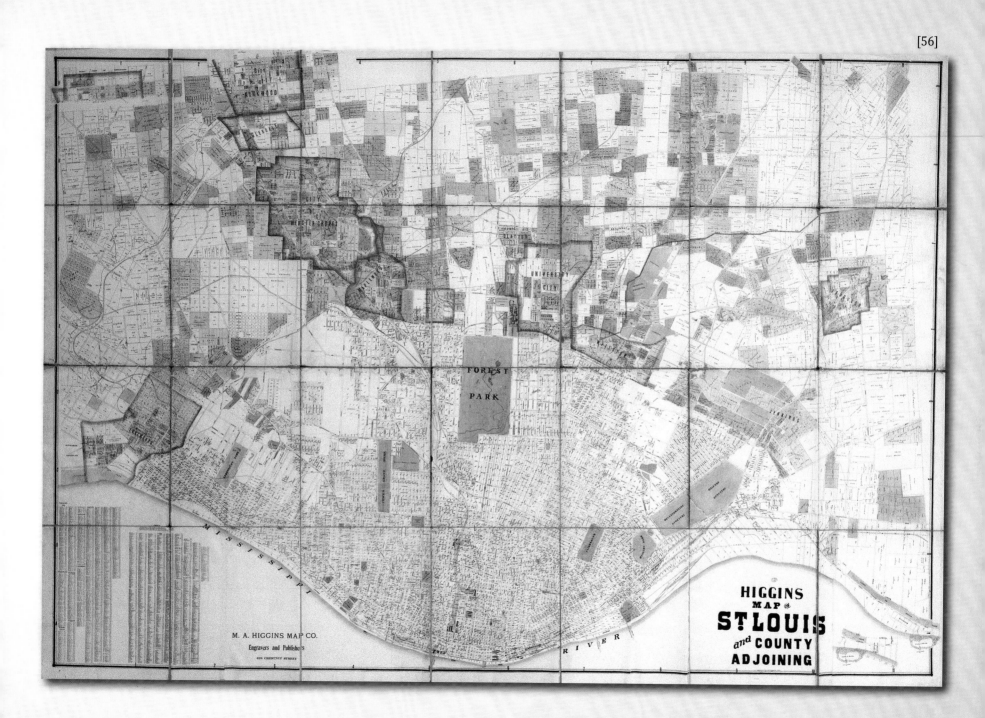

HIGGINS
MAP of
ST. LOUIS
and COUNTY
ADJOINING

M. A. HIGGINS MAP CO.
Engravers and Publishers
620 CHESTNUT STREET

57

Map of St. Louis and Vicinity. (St. Louis: Norgard Engineering Co., 1925) **[57a]**; with three plans from *Report on Rapid Transit for St. Louis.* (St. Louis: Board of Aldermen, 1926): *"Street Car Movements"* **[57b]**; *"Surface Car Subways with Rerouted Car Lines"* **[Fig. a]**; and a proposed *"River Front Plaza and Rapid Transit Terminals"* **[Fig. b]**; and with two plans to develop the central and northern river fronts of St. Louis from the late 1920s, proposed by Harland Bartholomew and the City Plan Commission, **[Figs. c, d]**: *"A Proposed Development of the Northern River Front, Saint Louis"* and *"The New Front of the Business District of St. Louis Drawn by Fred Graf."*

Norgard produced one of the first large scale engineering company maps for St. Louis, later perfected by the street map indexes subsequently created for St. Louis by Elbring Survey Associates and Wunnenberg Engineering Co. This thorough map presents a picture of a divided community, however, with segregated schools, for example, prominently noted; also a city slowing down—street cars moved the public but at a great cost of congestion, hence a great push of a rapid transit system—even the river front could be magnificently redeveloped—in the mind's eye—in this "growing pains" era of such a large, urban area.

[Fig. a]

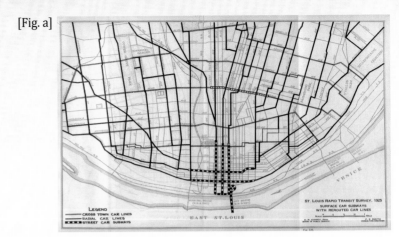

[Fig. b]

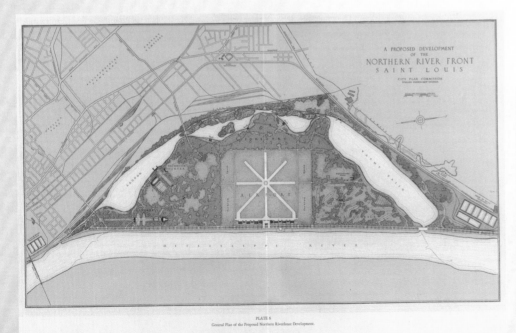

[Fig. c]

[Fig. d]

[57a]

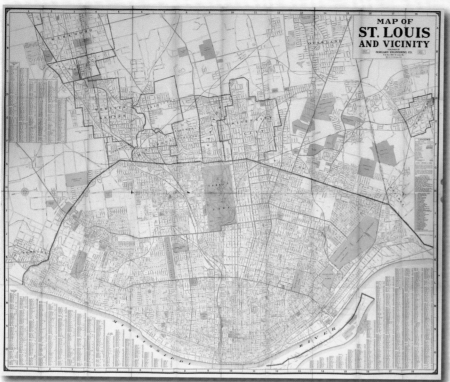

[57b]

123

58

Map of the City of St. Louis. St. Louis: Board of Public Service, 1931 [revision, 1936] **[58a]** [detail]; with *Report of the Transportation Survey Commission (St. Louis: Board of Aldermen, 1930)* **[58b, c]**: *"Map A: Time Zones for Street Car and Feeder Bus Lines Based on Service and Routing"* and *"Map Showing Existing Track Layout in Downtown St. Louis".*

The Public Service commission map and the large street map to follow in the next section (Item 59) show the down-to-earth concerns of an American city in the Model A era, still competing with street cars, tracks and even horse drawn conveyances. These are not grand planning maps for projects never attempted, but working maps for a city surviving the Great Depression era.

8th and Olive from rooftops.

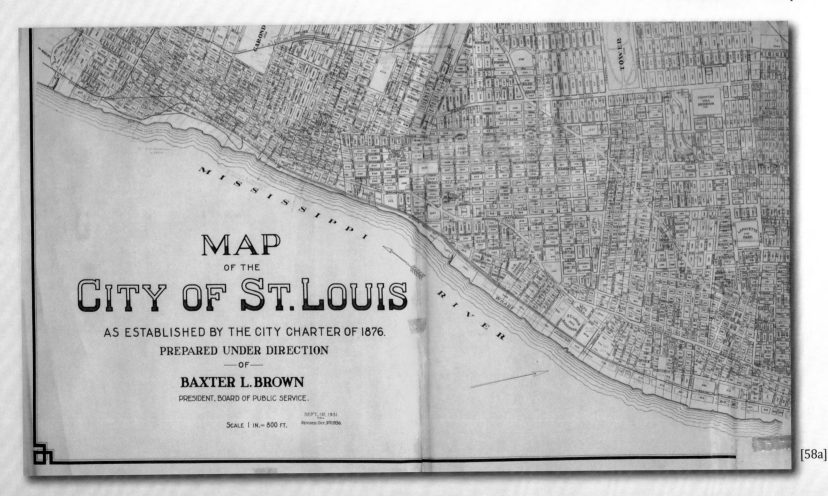

MAP
OF THE
CITY OF ST. LOUIS
AS ESTABLISHED BY THE CITY CHARTER OF 1876.
PREPARED UNDER DIRECTION
—OF—
BAXTER L. BROWN
PRESIDENT, BOARD OF PUBLIC SERVICE.

SEPT. 1ST. 1931.
SCALE 1 IN. = 800 FT.   REVISED OCT. 9TH. 1936.

[58a]

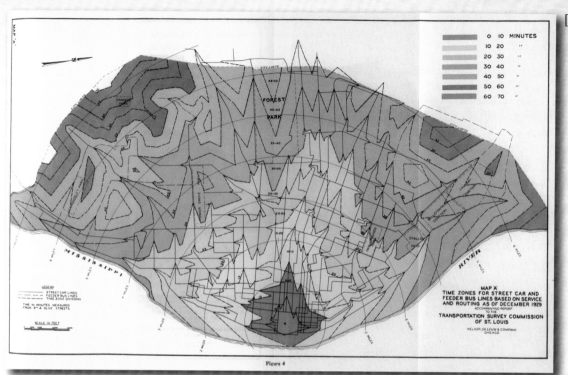

MAP "A"
TIME ZONES FOR STREET CAR AND
FEEDER BUS LINES BASED ON SERVICE
AND ROUTING AS OF DECEMBER 1929
ACCOMPANYING REPORT
TO THE
TRANSPORTATION SURVEY COMMISSION
OF ST. LOUIS
KELKER, DE LEUW & COMPANY
CHICAGO

Figure 4

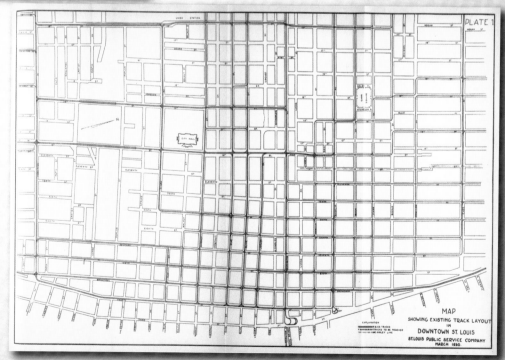

PLATE 1

MAP
SHOWING EXISTING TRACK LAYOUT
IN
DOWNTOWN ST. LOUIS
ST. LOUIS PUBLIC SERVICE COMPANY
MARCH 1930.

59 ***Cram's Street Map of Saint Louis County.*** Indianapolis: George F. Cram, 1939 **[59]**.

St. Louis at the end of the Depression and on the eve of American entry into World War II.

Part Five:

Roadways and Railways and Modern Urban Issues—Pathways and Plans to the Future

St. Louis was a town to be studied and planned increasingly in this transportation crossroads and often maps were used to project urban development and renewal such as the important Elbring and Wunnenberg engineering survey maps from the late thirties to the 1950s, which projected ownership patterns onto real estate trends for the first time for city planners, development agencies and investors **[Fig. a, b]**; or as rehabilitation of historic areas blossomed, again elaborate charts were brought out to make the process conform to a city planning code steeped in historic tradition, as seen in neighborhood maps of Lafayette Square and the Central West End **[Fig. c, d]**.

[Fig. a]

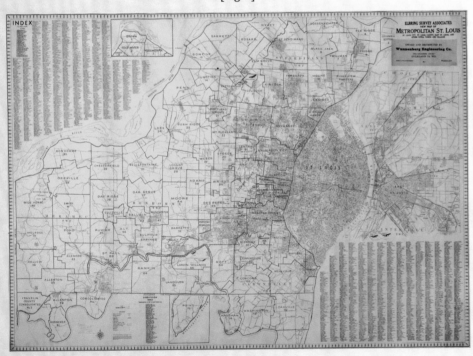

[Fig. b]

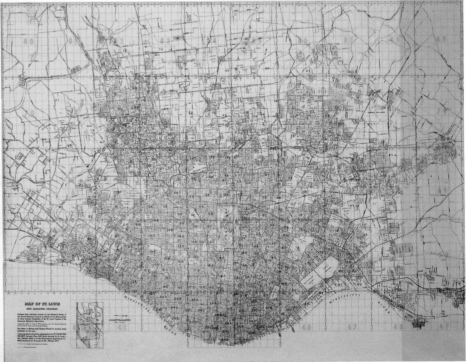

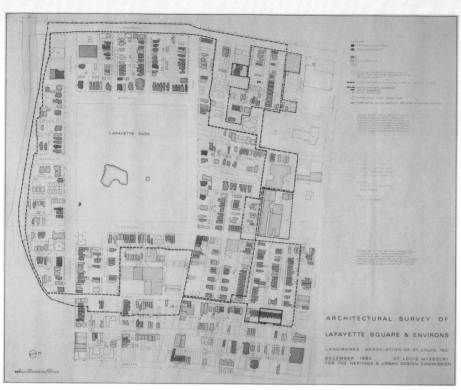

[Fig. c]

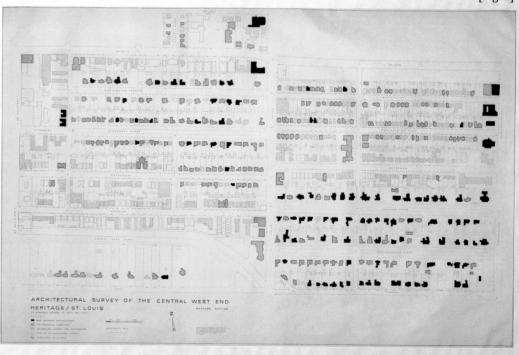

[Fig. d]

129

60

Aerial Map of St. Louis and Vicinity. St. Louis: Adult Education Council of Greater St. Louis, 1946 **[60a]**; with two maps from *St. Louis after World War II. (St. Louis: City Plan Commission, 1942): "Average Block Age of Residential Buildings"* **[60b]**; and *"Substandard Dwelling Units"* **[60c]** and with *Progress Report on the Jefferson Expansion Memorial. (St. Louis; 1940)* **[Fig. a]**.

During the 1940s two different St. Louis communities emerge from plans, dreams and realities. Here in *"The Aerial Map"* is presented a very old, historic city, filled with model schools, universities and museums and other educational resources that had become the envy of the central United States region, but here also in planning commission documents were seen the problems of decay and neglect—deferred maintenance—that a busy, ancient city inherently contends with on a proposed pathway to progress. The effort to rebuild the river front, as well as plan a national park for the Jefferson National Expansion Memorial had been stalled during years of land clearance—obviously these maps reveal that there was great potential but only realized in slow increments.

[Fig. a]

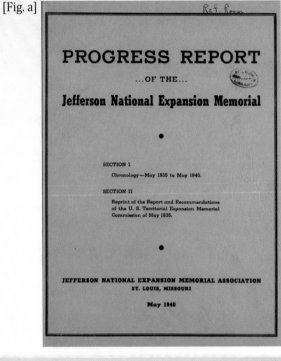

City Plan Commission aerial photograph of the St. Louis Riverfront before demolition began at mid-century for the Jefferson National Expansion Memorial.

[60a]

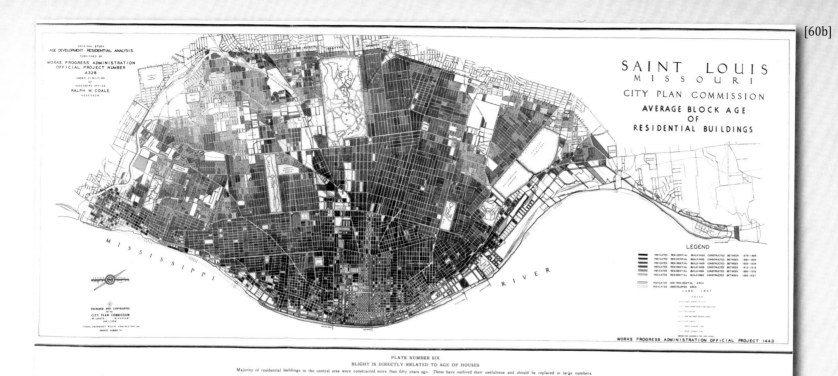

PLATE NUMBER SIX
BLIGHT IS DIRECTLY RELATED TO AGE OF HOUSES
Majority of residential buildings in the central area were constructed more than fifty years ago. These have outlived their usefulness and should be replaced in large numbers.

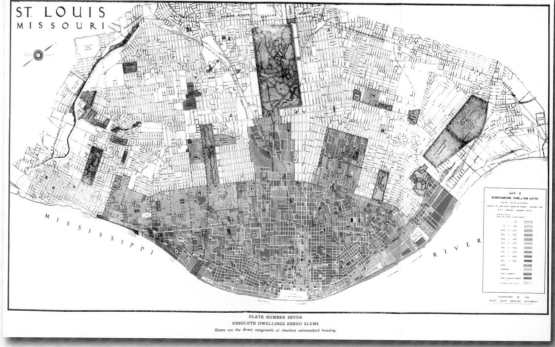

PLATE NUMBER SEVEN
OBSOLETE DWELLINGS BREED SLUMS
Slums are the direct outgrowth of obsolete substandard housing.

61 Harland Bartholomew. **Map of Comprehensive City Plan of Saint Louis, Missouri** from Comprehensive City Plan, Saint Louis Missouri. (St. Louis: City Plan Commission: 1947) **[61a]**; two maps from the plan: *"Neighborhoods & Industrial Districts"* **[Fig. a]**; and *"Obsolete and Blighted Districts"* **[Fig. b]**; and with *"Vertical View of the Program Site"* **[61b]**; and *"The Plan of the Memorial Area and its Immediate Surroundings"* **[61c]** from *Program of the Open Two-Stage Architectural Competition to Select an Architect and a Design to be Recommended to the Department of the Interior for the Jefferson National Expansion Memorial"* (St. Louis: 1947).

Bartholomew was one of the pioneers of American city planning, viewing a city as a system of many physical and economic systems. He held the post of City Planner in St. Louis for decades, the first permanent position as such in America. He was a city planner in the all encompassing age of the automobile, seeming to demand a broad, futuristic philosophy and sweep, and he went about recommending whole scale land clearance and demolition of "blighted districts" through zoning laws and eminent domain, and valued city lands as useful or less than productive based on amount of taxes recovered from the cost of city services delivered. His views for St. Louis were revolutionary for their time and seemed to work well in a prosperous environment but took generations to be reconsidered, as other viewpoints to land use and historical preservation in the urban landscape became valued as well in public policy debates. His impact on St. Louis, from neighborhood development, to easements and zoning laws, from subdivision planning to railroad location, from street widening to slum clearance has been profound. It is interesting that the fullest statements of his planning philosophy, these 1947 documents, employed maps and views of the city back to the 1790s for inspiration and reconsideration of what the city had become and was to become.

Demolition completed for the St. Louis Archground.

[Fig. a]

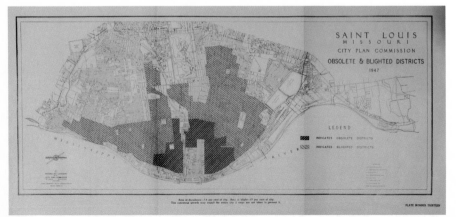

[Fig. b]

[61a]

[61b]

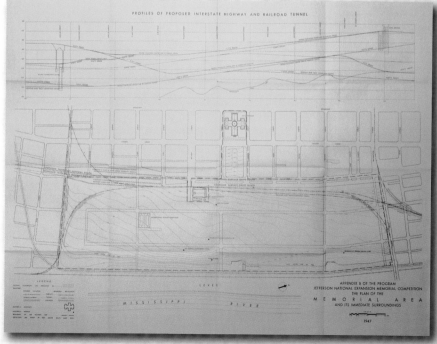

[61c]

62

United States Department of the Interior Geological Survey. *Selected Quadrangle maps of the Survey for the St. Louis Metropolitan Area.* Washington:1954 **[62]**; with an image of city planners using a chart map of St. Louis (such as this spliced composite map) from the 1950 *Annual Report* of the St. Louis Housing Authority **[Fig. a]**.

The U.S. Geological Survey, as massive an institution as it was to become, actually started as a cost saving measure to reign in such considered excessive activities as the simultaneous surveys of the American west of the later 19th century by Wheeler, Hayden, Powell and others. It grew into a meticulous and painstaking topographical undertaking crucial to an American's sense of place, location and movement to the present day.

Bus and streetcar strike, 1950.

[Fig. a]

Water trough at 3rd and Washington, 1937.

134

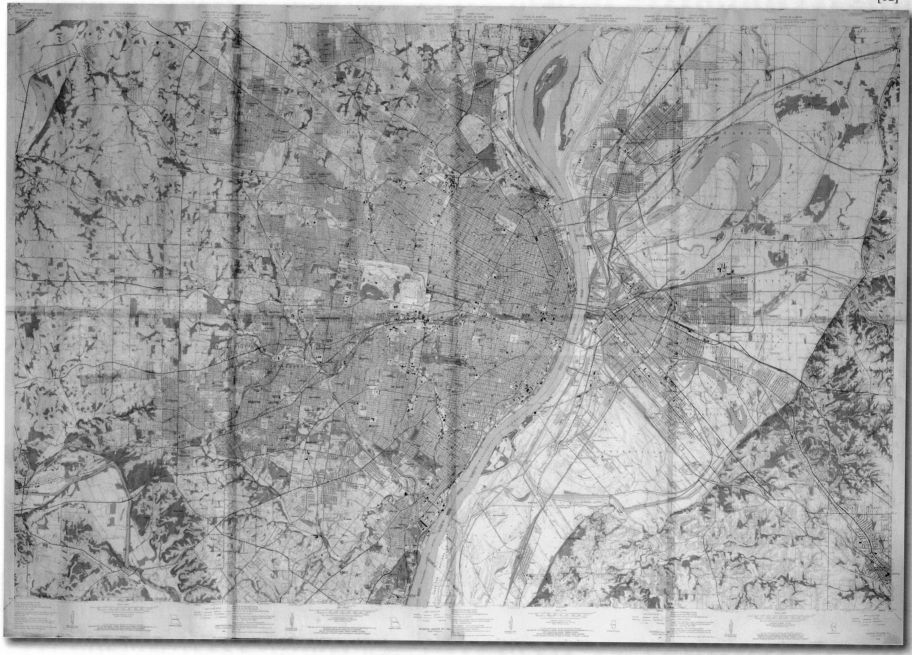

63 The Roads:

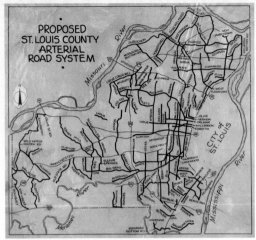

Auto Road Map, St. Louis & Vicinity. (Chicago: McNally, undated, [ca.: 1920]. **[63a]**; with two maps showing alternate locations for the routing of the Mark Twain Expressway, *(Expressway Plan for St. Louis and Adjacent Area prepared by Malcolm Elliott, St. Louis: 1951)* **[63b]**; and Interstate 44 *(Report on Alternate Locations of Interstate 44 in the City and County of St. Louis, Missouri, Missouri State Highway Dept., 1959)* **[63c]** through St. Louis; with a working document for a planning meeting *"Proposed St. Louis County Arterial Road System"* **[Fig. a]**; and *"General Highway Map",* St. Louis County, (prepared in 1957 by the U.S. Dept. of Commerce and the Missouri State Highway Department) **[63d]** with map of *"Metropolitan St. Louis"* published by the St. Louis Chamber of Commerce, showing many proposed expressways nearing completion in 1968 **[Fig. b]** and with a cartoon for the St. Louis Post Dispatch by Daniel Fitzpatrick, *"Downtown St. Louis, Traffic Tangle, Slums: Progress or Decay"* **[Fig. c]** and **[Fig. d]**: a contemporary early road map from St. Louis published by H. W. Gross.

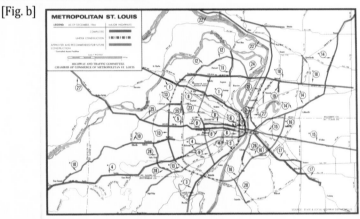

[Fig. b]

These selected roadways of the twentieth century across St. Louis City and County show generations-long struggles against traffic congestion. As seen in an early road map, traffic moving east-west necessarily was snarled in downtown St. Louis, both directions, due to the few bridges in service for automobiles, and the fact that the US Highway system for many years did not bypass center city areas, but routed all traffic through the densest areas of population. This led to a critical situation in St. Louis and thus no one was very alarmed from a neighborhood or preservation standpoint when the first expressways for the alleviation of these traffic woes cut through or even demolished whole scale communities, slicing through the city the way a hot knife passes through butter. The trade-off was felt worth it.

[Fig. c]

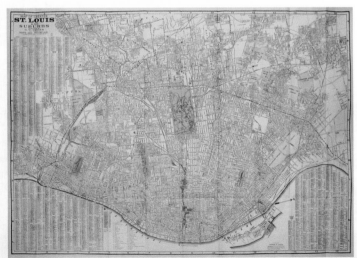

[Fig. d]

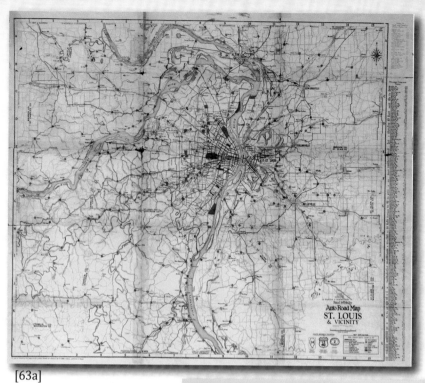
[63a]

[63d]

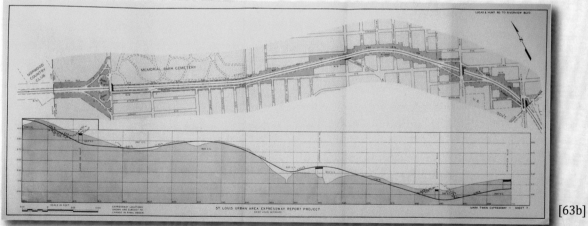
[63b]

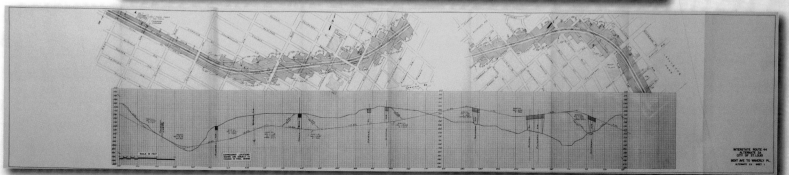
[63c]

The Rails:

Plat of St. Louis and Vicinity, Showing Railway System of the Terminal R. R. Association of St. Louis, St. Louis Merchants Bridge Terminal Ry. Co., Wiggens Ferry Company. (St. Louis: 1928) **[63e]**; with *"Tourist's Trolley Map of St. Louis and Environs" (St. Louis, United Railways Company, 1915)* **[63f]** with *"City of St. Louis, Frisco Line Terminals"* **[63g]**; and with four additional plats of the rails coming into St. Louis: 1923 **[Fig. e]**; 1932 **[Fig. f]**; an undated map from the same era, but with a different perspective focusing on Union Station alone in relation to distance from the river **[Fig. g]**; and a contemporary Union Pacific Railroad Map: *"St. Louis and Vicinity, AEI Locations"* **[Fig. h]**; and with time tables of various railways coming to St. Louis; *Frisco, 1955* **[Fig. i]**; *Missouri Pacific Lines, 1960* **[Fig. j]**; *M-K-T Katy Railroad, 1946* **[Fig. k]**; and *Cotton Belt Route, 1929* **[Fig. l]** and the original map of the St. Louis' first metro rapid transit system, ca. 1995, *"Welcome Aboard MetroLink"* **[63h]**.

St. Louis had from the 1860s one of the most highly developed rail systems of any American city and to this day the freight yards and various lines coming through the city stand testament to that heritage and the new chapters being written on the railways in the United States. By comparison to the congestion the automobile endured in St. Louis for much of the twentieth century, by the 1920s at the height of the passenger era St. Louis' many rail bridges, and the yards and terminals, stations and depots across the city made it railroad friendly, for visitors and commuters using the streetcars, to cross country travelers passing through the glorious architectural landmark of Union Station. When the metro system came about rather late in the history of St. Louis, long since having become a "car town" due to the success of the expressway system, it was as if a revelation occurred—the old track and routes were used to lead passengers from Scott Air Force Base on the east side of the river to Lambert International Airport far to the northwest and became a virtual tour of the history of the city. Citizens took this trip over and over again, remembering the legends and stories of a community so long tied to these steel pathways.

[Fig. e]

[Fig. f]

[Fig. g]

[Fig. h]

[Fig. i]

[Fig. j]

[Fig. k]

[Fig. l]

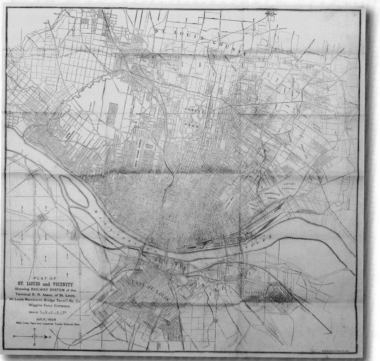

[63e]

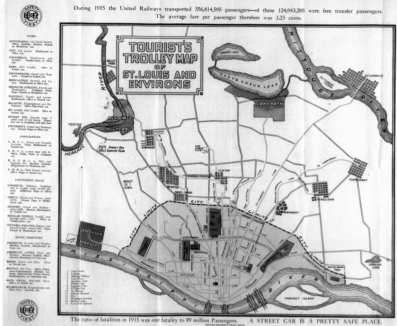

[63f]

During 1915 the United Railways transported 356,814,595 passengers—of these 124,043,205 were free transfer passengers. The average fare per passenger therefore was 3.23 cents.

TOURISTS TROLLEY MAP OF ST. LOUIS AND ENVIRONS

The ratio of fatalities in 1915 was one fatality to 89 million Passengers. A STREET CAR IS A PRETTY SAFE PLACE.

FRISCO LINE TERMINALS SHOWN IN RED.

CITY OF ST. LOUIS
SHEET Nº 1
SCALE 500:1"

[63g]

[63h]

WELCOME ABOARD METROLINK

Lambert Airport Main
Lambert Airport East
North Hanley
UM-St. Louis North
UM-St. Louis South
Rock Road
Wellston
Delmar
Forest Park
Central West End
Grand
Union Station
Kiel Center
Busch Stadium
8th & Pine
Convention Center
Laclede's Landing
East Riverfront
5th & Missouri
Emerson Park
Jackie Joyner-Kersee Ctr.
Washington Park
Fairview Heights
Memorial Hospital
Swansea
Belleville
College

P Park-Ride Lot
○ Ride Free Zone

Ride Free Zone

Ride Free Zone
11:30 a.m. – 1:30 p.m. Monday - Friday

64 Theodore Link. **Plan of Forest Park.** (St. Louis: Daly, 1876) **[64a]**; with *"A Topographical Map of Forest Park"* by Camille Dry (St. Louis: Studley, 1876) **[64b]**; and with *"Major County Parks"* (St. Louis, 1966) **[Fig. a]**; and with *"Map of Sewer Districts"* (St. Louis, 1949) **[Fig. b]**; with Mimi Garstang's *"Underground Coal and Clay Mines in the City of St. Louis, Missouri"* (Rolla: Mo. Dept. of Natural Resources, 1987) **[64c]**; and with an undated (ca: 1930s) *"Plan Showing Grade Crossings and Separations, St. Louis, Mo."* **[64d]**; and with *"Regional Bikeways of Metro St. Louis"* (Madison County Transit: 2007) **[Fig. c]** and with *"28th Ward"* (St. Louis: Board of Elections, 1959) **[Fig d]** and a plan for *"Tower Grove Crossing"* (1962) **[Fig. e]**.

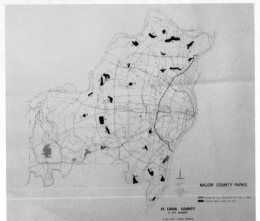

[Fig. a]

These maps show the development of community through the lens of special places, like parks; special concerns, as safety issues surrounding the vast rail system of the city at the busy and at times dangerous crossings; and needs, such as the later push for recreation not bounded by parks, but as far as a bicycle trail would lead. Yet Forest Park itself has been such a focal point for city and county for so many generations, that even the election map for the 28th Voting Ward would naturally use the Park to orient residents in that electoral division. Some plans, like interstates whizzing through the heart of Tower Grove, were gratefully tempered by an appreciation for this early green space in the heart of the city.

[Fig. b]

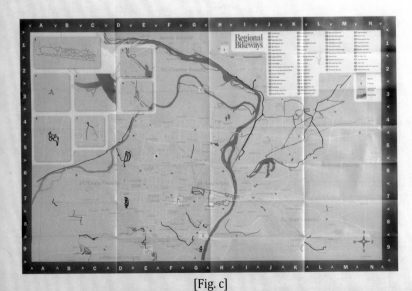

[Fig. c]

[Fig. d]

[Fig. e]

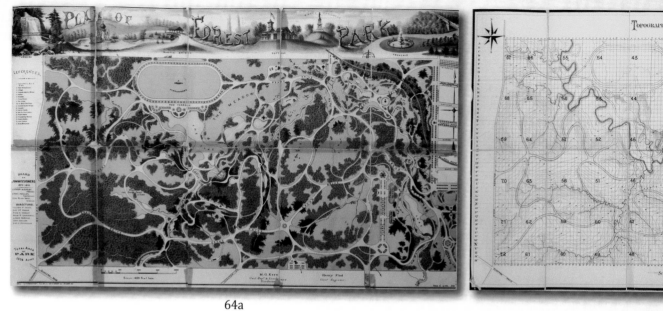

64a

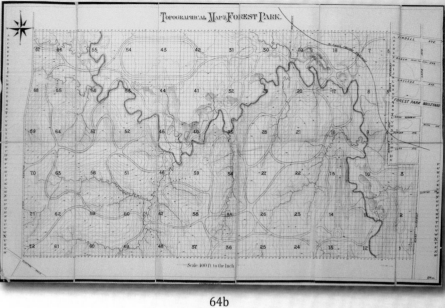

64b

64c

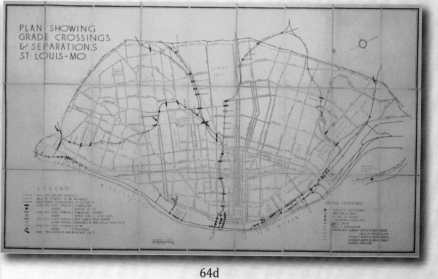

64d

141

65

Neighborhoods. (St. Louis: Community Development Agency, 1991) **[65a]**; with a map of *"City of Kirkwood"* (St. Louis: Graf, 1908) **[65b]**; and other early neighborhood plans: *"Woodland and Glendale"*, 1893 **[Fig. a]**; *"Clemens Place"*, undated **[Fig. b]**; *"Shield's"*, 1893 **[Fig. c]**; *"Crown Point"*, 1905 **[Fig. d]**; *"Maplewood"*, 1909 **[Fig. e]**; *"Richmond Heights"*, 1909 **[Fig. f]** and one of the earliest planned communities developed west of the Mississippi to take advantage of rails and trade just to the north in St. Louis *"Missouri City"* (Boston: ca. 1840) **[65c]**; and with architectural elevations of St. Louis suburban houses from the 1930s **[Fig. g, h, i]**; and with a schematic for the City Planning Commission rules for set back from the neighborhood thoroughfare. **[65d]**; also with the original prospectus for Westroads Shopping Center ca. 1961; and a plan for Northland Shopping Center, mid 1950s. **[Fig. j, k]**.

St. Louis is a city of neighborhoods and St. Louis County a world of suburbs and municipalities, long ago planned and designed with fine houses and shopping centers intended to create a suburban paradise. A place like Westroads, now the St. Louis Galleria, was designed as its developers put it, as a "crossroads of the County," a community gathering place.

[Fig. a]

[Fig. b]

[Fig. c]

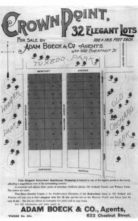

[Fig. d]

[Fig. e]   [Fig. f]

[Fig. i]

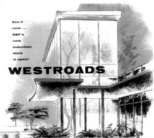

[Fig. j]

[Fig. g]   [Fig. h]

[Fig. k]

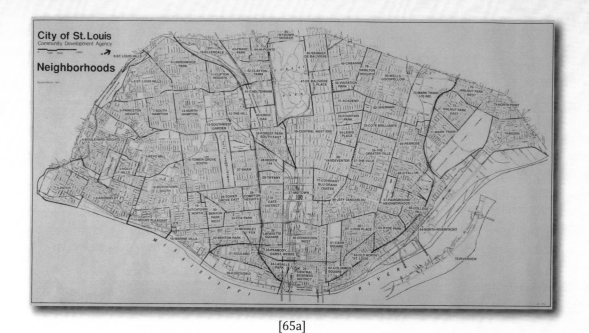

[65a]

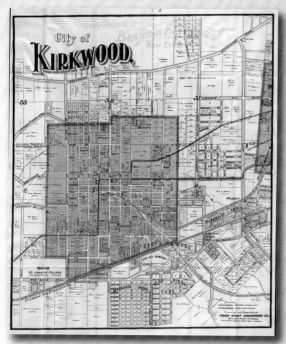

[65b]

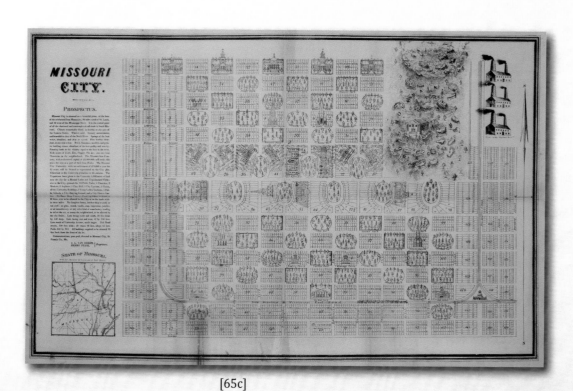

[65c]

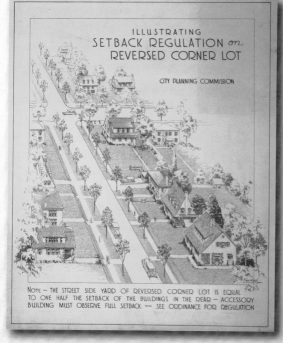

[65d]

143

66

Globe Democrat Bicentennial St. Louis Metropolitan Map. (1964) **[66a]**; with Charles R. Flachmann's and Frank Nudersher's splendid "Pictographic" maps of St. Louis **[66 b, c]**; and with perhaps one of the last graphic schematic views of St. Louis, which in its day had seen hundreds of such portraits, "St. Louis, 1985" **[Fig. a]**.

The Globe Democrat map was a wonderfully interactive, pre-digital map—too complicated to be practical, but full of information on Laclède's and Chouteau's fabled, just turned 200 year old city full of civic pride and the landmarks of the period.

[Fig. a]

St. Louis 1985

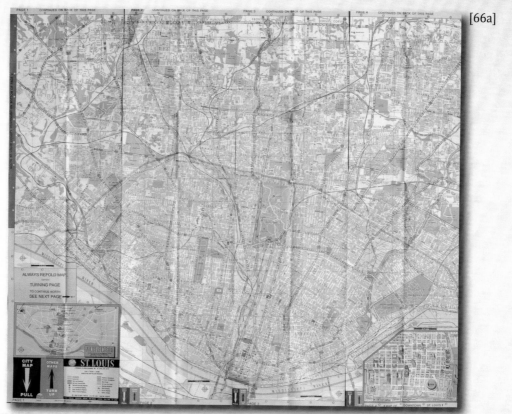

[66a]

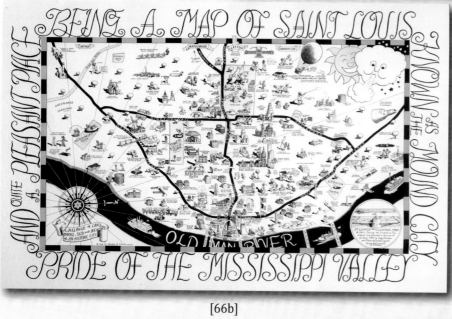

[66b]

[66c]

145

67

Townships of St. Louis County and City. St. Louis County Planning Commission, 1965. **[67a]**; *"The New St. Louis."* (St. Louis: Chamber of Commerce, 1964) **[Fig. a]**; and with two prophetic charts showing how a great amount of planning had indeed come to pass: *"St. Louis Post-Dispatch Special Progress Section"* [newspaper special section] (Sunday, May 7, 1961) **[Fig. b]**; and a chart from the City Plan Commission, *"Land Use Plan"* (1956) **[67b]**.

This is a working map with the creases and overuse to prove it of a time which shouts after the Bicentennial of the City, "The party's over, time to get down to work"; perhaps a map like this, coming from the *county* planning commission, is a glimpse of the future of today, with the first serious talks of city-county combination once more in the air.

[Fig. b]

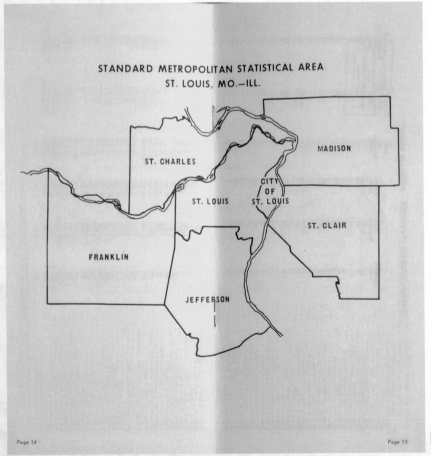

[Fig. a]

[67a]

TOWNSHIPS

MARCH 1965

FLORISSANT

SPANISH LAKE

AIRPORT

FERGUSON

ST. FERDINAND

MIDLAND

NORMANDY

WASHINGTON

CREVE COEUR

HADLEY

CLAYTON

LINCOLN

MERAMEC

BONHOMME

JEFFERSON

GRAVOIS

CONCORD

LEMAY

ST. LOUIS COUNTY

& CITY, MISSOURI

ST. LOUIS COUNTY PLANNING COMMISSION

[67b]

RESIDENTIAL
INDUSTRIAL
COMMERCIAL
METROPOLITAN SERVICE
COMMERCIAL DISTRICT
SHOPPING CENTER
OPEN RECREATION   10 ACRES or MORE
OTHER PUBLIC
& SEMI PUBLIC
CEMETERY
EXPRESSWAY or PARKWAY
ARTERIAL STREET

1956

ST. LOUIS
CITY PLAN
COMMISSION

LAND USE PLAN

68

Working Study Plans for CityArchRiver Project. (St. Louis: 2012-13) **[68 a]**; with two City Plan Commission charts, one from a *"Plan for Downtown St. Louis"* (1960) **[68b]**; and *"St. Louis Riverfront Development Plan"* (1967) **[68c]**.

These plans show a half century of concern for a city which needed connection with its life force, the Mississippi River. The earlier plans were ambitious ways to develop downtown and the riverfront west, north and south comprehensively. The newest plan look at a way to move and reconnect the city back easterly—to the river front itself.

St. Louis in the 1960s after enormous rebuilding based on decades of city planning.

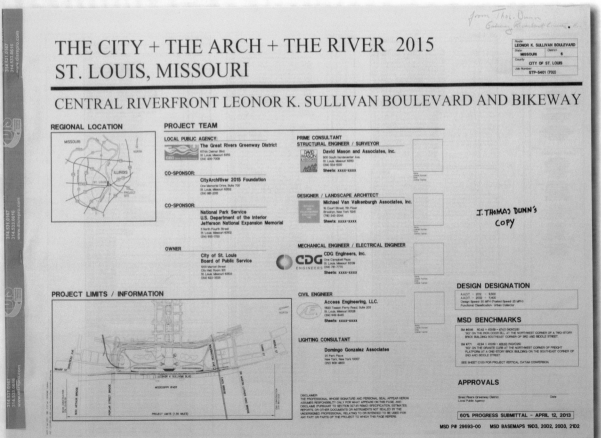

[68a]

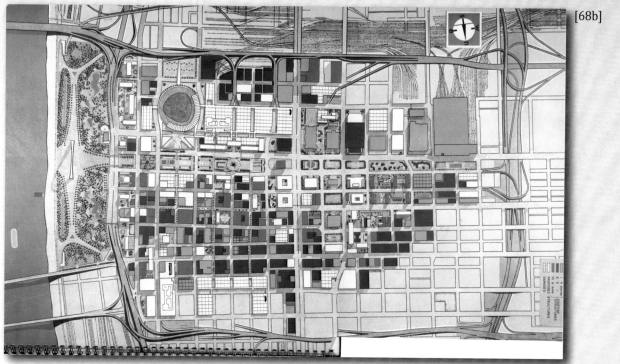

[68b]

[68c]

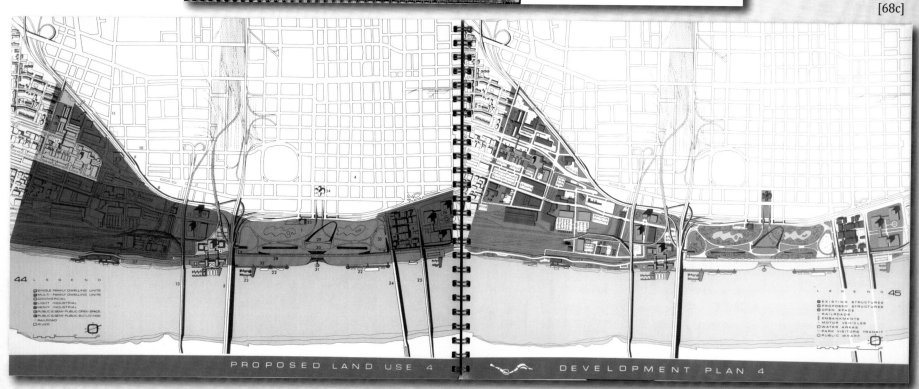

44 LEGEND
- SINGLE-FAMILY DWELLING UNITS
- MULTI-FAMILY DWELLING UNITS
- COMMERCIAL
- LIGHT INDUSTRIAL
- HEAVY INDUSTRIAL
- PUBLIC & SEMI-PUBLIC OPEN SPACE
- PUBLIC & SEMI-PUBLIC BUILDINGS
- RAILROAD
- RIVER

LEGEND 45
- EXISTING STRUCTURES
- PROPOSED STRUCTURES
- OPEN SPACE
- RAILROADS
- EMBANKMENTS
- MOTOR VEHICLES
- WATER AREAS
- PARK VISITORS TRANSIT
- PUBLIC WHARF

PROPOSED LAND USE 4   DEVELOPMENT PLAN 4

NASA Photo ISS038-E-024442. (2013) **[69]**.

A photograph taken December 7, 2013 from the Earth-orbiting International Space Station by one of the Expedition 38 crew on board of a night image of St. Louis, Missouri and East St. Louis, Illinois and the surrounding area of the ancient "Illinois country."

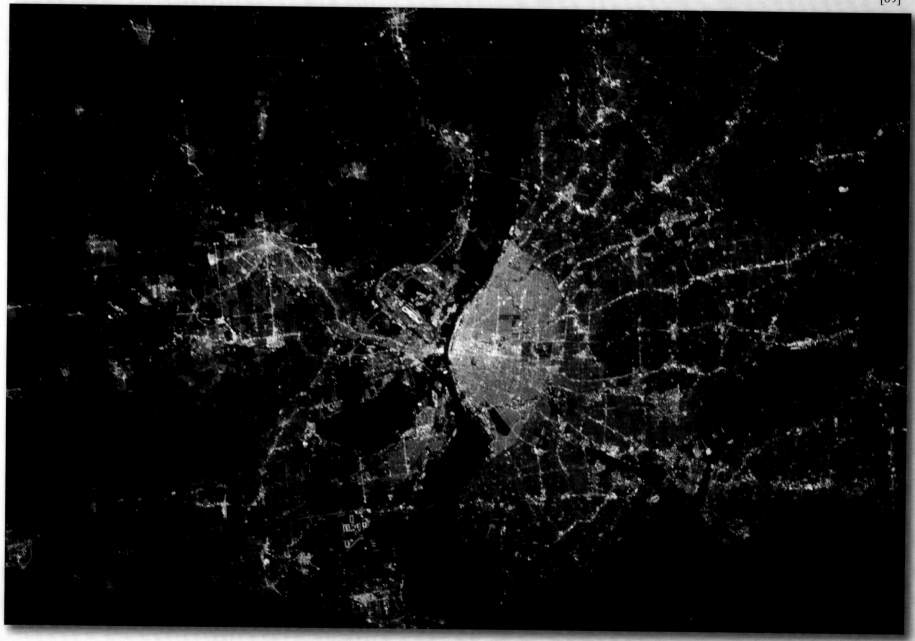

69

70

Metropolitan St. Louis and Vicinity. (St. Louis: Chamber of Commerce, 1964) **[70a]**; with *"St. Louis, MO and Vicinity,"* (St. Louis: Color-Art, 2014) **[70b]**; and with a map of the *"Port of St. Louis"* (St. Louis: ca. 1970) **[70c]**.

The two modern master perspectives related to mapping St. Louis. The two city maps from fifty years apart show an ever westerly course for population and settlement of millions of citizens referencing "St. Louis" as home. The second is the standard traveler's map distributed by Enterprise Leasing of St. Louis. The harbor map is a virtual late 20th history of an active and living port, one in existence for 250 years of North America's long, intricate and exuberant history.

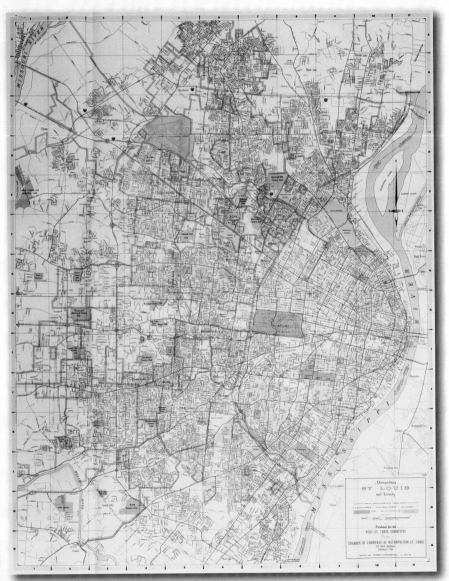

[70a]

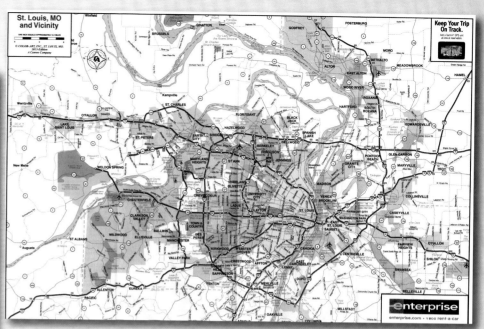

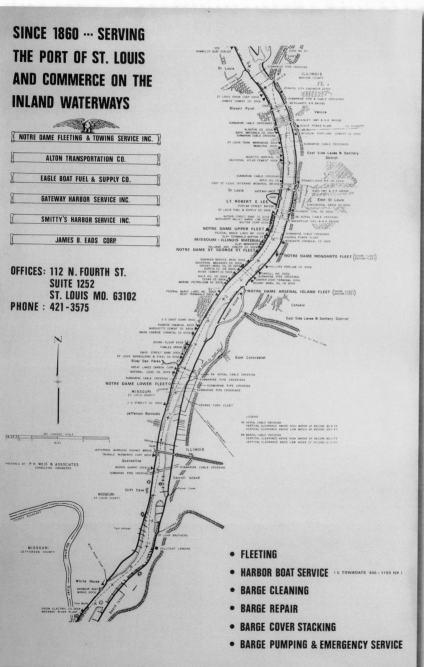

Afterword

At the end of World War II a plan was sent from St. Louis leaders to the United States Representative to the Preparatory Commissions for the United Nations, inviting him and that body to consider the St. Louis area as the future—and from the perspective of the St. Louis Chamber of Commerce and the Mayor's Office, quite logical—home of the United Nations. The maps from this invitation **[Fig. a, b]** show the "heartland state of mind", its boundless optimism and ambition, perfectly. This was a traditional stance, indicated repeatedly over the centuries. The UN invitation echoes the grand and quite serious local and national movement in the second half of the nineteenth century to move the United States capital to the banks of the Mississippi and to St. Louis. Time and again the strategic importance and the centrality of the St. Louis region at its meeting of the waters was understood to be quite very special. Long before St. Louis even existed, colonial empires knew that landscape. Early St. Louisans positioned the city to face the west for a local trading monopoly on all of this continent's natural resources. The first Americans instantly built a strong military presence here at Jefferson Barracks and went about creating a new metropolis for the new nation.

Two types of maps tell St. Louis' story well—those pinned to the river and the riverfront, such as the UN maps—St. Louis as a destination, a central lynchpin—and those showing St. Louis as the first point to somewhere else—specifically, the west. The vast map of the river system by Nicollet begins at St. Louis **[Fig. c]**; the Warren map of the *Pacific Railroad Surveys* does the same **[Fig. d]** as so many earlier maps had done for generations. The celebrated map of the region of the confluence by Nicolas de Finiels shows the city by the river, connected to it as a mother and child, but already with the first westerly roads leading to St. Charles and a new, boundless continent. **[Fig. e]**.

Two themes—the river and St. Louis through time, and the West and St. Louis—show the two views that a St. Louisan has about a place of storied legend and repute, his or her own city. In looking at the maps of the city, one can easily gain a notion as to how the city of St. Louis has been pinned to an American consciousness for 250 years in ways that only its maps can best reflect.

JNH

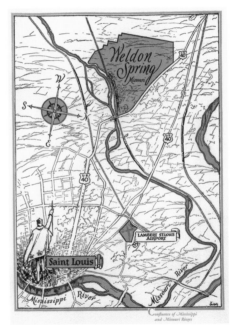

[Fig. a]

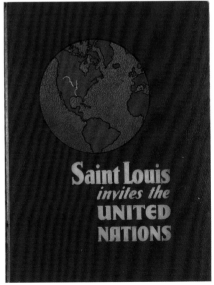

[Fig. b]

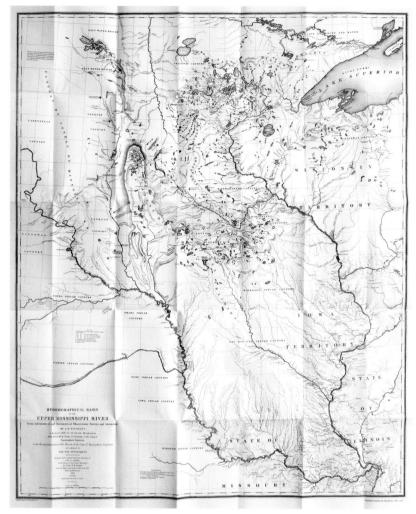

[Fig. c]

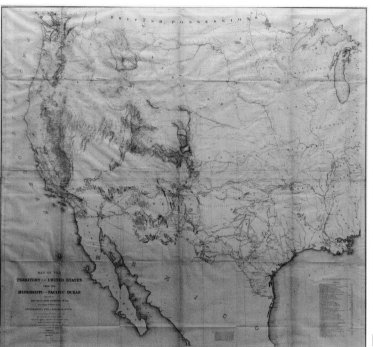

[Fig. d]

[Fig. e]

Service historique de la Défense; Château de Vincennes.

Selected Readings

F. L. Billon. *Annals of St. Louis in Its Early Days.* St. Louis: Nixon-Jones, 1886.

F. L. Billon. *Annals of St. Louis in its Territorial Days.* St. Louis: Nixon-John, 1889.

Paul E. Cohen. *Mapping the West.* New York: Rizzoli: 2002.

Mathew Erickson. "The Resuspended City." *The Believer* (Oct. 2013). pp 17-21.

John R. Hebert. *Panoramic Maps of Anglo-American Cities.* Washington: Library of Congress, 1974.

Harry M. Hogan. *This is Our St. Louis.* St. Louis: Knight, 1970.

Robert A. Holland. *The Mississippi River in Maps and Views.* New York: Rizzoli, 2008.

Alice C. Hudson and Barbara Cohen-Stratyner. *Heading West' Touring West; Mapmakers, Performing Arts and the American Frontier.* New York: New York Public Library, 2001.

Ben W. Huseman. *"Territories So Extensive and Fertile": The Louisiana Purchase.* Dallas: De Golyer Library, 2004.

Robert W. Karrow and David Buisseret. *Gardens of Delight; Maps and Travel Accounts of Illinois and the Great Lakes.* Chicago: The Newberry Library, 1984.

Peter J. Kastor. *William Clark's World; Describing America in an Age of Unknowns.* New Haven: Yale, 2011.

Richard S. Ladd. *Maps Showing Explorer's Routes, Trails, and Early Roads in the United States.* Washington: Library of Congress, 1962.

John Francis McDermott, ed. *Old Cahokia.* St. Louis: St. Louis Historical Documents Foundation, 1949.

John Francis McDermott, ed. *Philip Pittman's "The Present State of the Early Settlements on the Mississippi" (London, 1770).* Memphis: Memphis State University, 1977.

John Francis McDermott, ed. *Travelers on the Western Frontier.* Urbana: University of Illinois, 1970.

James B. Musick. *St. Louis as a Fortified Town.* St. Louis: Miller, 1941.

Charles E. Peterson. *Colonial St. Louis.* Tucson: Patrice Press, 1993.

John W. Reps. *St. Louis Illustrated.* Columbia: University of Missouri Press, 1989.

The Jay T. Snider Collection of Historical Americana. Sale 1614, June 21, 2005. New York: Christie's, 2005.

Frances Hurd Stadler. *St. Louis: From Laclède to Land Clearance.* St. Louis: KSD, 1962.

The Frank S. Streeter Library. Sale 1820, April 16, 17, 2007. St. Louis: Christie's, 2007.

Charles Van Ravenswaay, ed. *St. Louis: A Fond Look Back.* St. Louis: First National Bank, 1956.

Charles Van Ravenswaay. *St. Louis: An Informal History of the City and Its People, 1764-1865.* St. Louis: Missouri Historical Society, 1991.

Norbury L. Wayman. *Physical Growth of the City of St. Louis.* St. Louis: City Plan Commission, 1969.

Index of Catalogue Entries

ONE THOUSAND COPIES

Mapping
St. Louis History:

An Exhibition of Historic Maps, Rare Books
and Images Commemorating the
250th Anniversary of the Founding of St. Louis

PRINTED IN SEPTEMBER 2014
AT WORLD PRESS, INC., ST. LOUIS, MISSOURI.

DESIGN AND TYPESETTING: PATRICIA ARCHER
PHOTOGRAPHY: AUGUST JENNEWEIN
ON 80# SILK
TYPEFACE: LIBERTY; CAMBRIA

New Orleans Packet.

Carondelet Ferry.

Wisconsin Raft for Carondelet.

Workhouse

ARSENAL ISLAND

U.S. Arsenal

ROSS' NEW MAP OF THE City of St. Louis.

A COMPLETE STRANGERS GUIDE,

SHOWING ALL THE STREETS, STREET-

PROMINENT BUILDINGS, PARKS,

RAILWAYS &c.

Published by

E. H. ROSS.

Nº 313 Locust St.

St. Louis,

1871

Mississippi Race between Lee & Natchez.

Club Boat.